BOOKS BY JOHN GASPARD

The Como Lake Players Mysteries
ACTING CAN BE MURDER
DYING TO AUDITION
REHEARSED TO DEATH

The Eli Marks Mystery Series
THE AMBITIOUS CARD (#1)
THE BULLET CATCH (#2)
THE MISER'S DREAM (#3)
THE LINKING RINGS (#4)
THE FLOATING LIGHT BULB (#5)
THE ZOMBIE BALL (#6)
THE MAGIC SQUARE (#7)
THE SELF-WORKING TRICK (#8)

Stand-Alone Novels
THE SWORD & MR. STONE
A CHRISTMAS CARL
THE GREYHOUND OF THE BASKERVILLES
THE RIPPEROLOGISTS

Filmmaking Books
FAST, CHEAP AND UNDER CONTROL
FAST, CHEAP AND WRITTEN THAT WAY
TELL THEM IT'S A DREAM SEQUENCE
WOMEN MAKE MOVIES

WOMEN MAKE MOVIES

INTERVIEWS WITH WOMEN IN THE INDUSTRY

JOHN GASPARD

PART I
THE DIRECTORS

AMY HECKERLING ON "FAST TIMES AT RIDGEMONT HIGH" AND "CLUELESS"

What was it that got you into filmmaking?

AMY: I've always loved movies, as a kid, forever. I'm watching one right now.

What are you watching?

AMY: *Bye Bye Birdie.*

When you first started wanting to make movies, what path was available to you?

AMY: I didn't realize that there was a path. Then when I felt like I can't NOT do this, I have to do it, there were film schools. But there were only a couple, a handful of them. There was UCLA, USC, the School of Visual Arts and NYU. And I had my heart set on NYU.

Why NYU?

AMY: Well, first of all, I couldn't afford to pay tuition and pay to live somewhere. So that took care of California. The School of Visual

Arts was a vocational school really, and I wanted to go to a university.

NYU was less connected to the show biz community than the California schools, but there was a gritty artiness to the movies they were trying to make and I appreciated that. It was a better fit for me, I was happy there.

What did you do after film school?

AMY: Well, I took my little movies and, even though they had won awards, I didn't feel like I was going to go to a company making movies and say, "Look at this," and then they would make my movies. So I said, "I need something better to show people." At the time, there were fewer people involved in the industry and it was much tougher.

Now, with all the equipment people have, you can make a feature for no money and use that as a calling card.

So I felt like I need a better calling card, so I went to The American Film Institute, where we could make much slicker, more professional-looking movies and have more access to the industry.

How tough was it to get into AFI then?

AMY: Everybody at NYU tried and only my cameraman and I got in.

What did you do at AFI?

AMY: Associates make videos, which I was not so happy with – I was a film lover. There was a big difference between what videos looked like and what films looked like.

And then your second year you can make a short film. So I made a short film and showed it to the studios. Actually, I had a screening at AFI and we sent invitations to agents and who ever you knew who knew somebody. And one of the people was David Gersch, from The Gersch Agency. He was a kid whose father had an agency.

So he showed it to some people, and I had a meeting at Warner Brothers. Then I pitched them something and they liked it, so then I was writing.

The thing that I wrote went into turnaround at Warner Brothers when they got new executives, and then it was at Universal, but it never got made there. Then it was at MGM and they were going to make it, when David Begelman was there, but then there was an actors' strike. In the interim, they found a similar project with big stars attached, so they said that it was an act of god that they couldn't do mine, force majeure.

It was an act of god that there was another similar script?

AMY: That's what they said. So we had worked all this time for nothing.

So what was your next move?

AMY: A guy I knew showed me a script. It was *Fast Times At Ridgemont High*. It was Art Linson. At Universal, I had an office next to him. He had shown me other scripts to see what I thought and we'd talk about stuff. And I thought that was what he was doing with this script, wanting to know what I thought of it.

And what did you think of it?

AMY: I thought that these kids – a couple of them have jobs at a strip of stores on the street in a small town and others didn't have jobs – and I said, "What if you put it all in a mall?" Because the mall was like the soda shop of the 1980s. And then you'd have the people working there and the people coming there and you could have more people work – because I think kids should work.

So he said, "That's great. What else?" And I said, "There's all these funny things that different people do and then there's this wacky guy Spicoli. Why don't you give these things to him to do?"

How did you get the job directing *Fast Times*?

AMY: They called and said "Do you want to direct it?" I was thrilled – I really wanted to direct. And then I met Cameron (Crowe), who I loved. And then we were doing it. We started working on the script and he was awesome. He's Cameron Crowe. He's amazing.

Tell me how you went about casting the movie, because it's brilliantly cast.

AMY: Well, thank you. One thing that always annoyed me about high school movies – although as I watch *Bye, Bye Birdie* it doesn't seem to annoy me – was that I always felt that they were grown-ups dressed in high-top sneakers and that makes you a teenager.

I wanted to have real kids because the point of *Fast Times* was that things were too fast, they were too young for things that were happening. So they had to really look young. They couldn't look like little grown-ups. They had to be children.

But then as we were going through the casting process, first of all you're limited because they have to be over eighteen. And Art Linson said something pretty brilliant to me: "You won't be unhappy if you just go with the talent. So if somebody looks ten years old and they're eighteen, that's great, but if they're not talented, you're not going to be happy. And if somebody is a genius actor – like Sean Penn and Forest Whitaker – you will be happy." So I did what he said.

That movie was shot in 35 days, without a very long pre-production period and not a very long post. I mean, that was a cheap movie. It was a $5 million dollar, 35-day movie.

What was it like for you on your first day on the set?

AMY: It was terrifying because I had to shoot a car driving by and I didn't know how big it should be. I knew where the camera should be, I just didn't know how big the car should be, how fast it should go, how long I should follow it for. But then I shot that and we were just shooting. You know, like everything, the first step's the hardest, even if the first step is nothing.

So what happened career-wise after *Fast Times* came out?

AMY: I had a lot of meetings with everybody who had a "virgin" script.

Was there something in particular you wanted to do?

AMY: I didn't get to do something I wanted because I still felt like I had to do what they wanted – as far as scripts they wanted to make – otherwise it would take forever and it would never happen. But I definitely didn't want to do another "girl loses her virginity" movie. There's tons of those.

What led you to write *Clueless*?

I had written a movie called *Rat Race*, which was based on a French movie, *Mon oncle d'Amérique*. It was developed at Disney and they kept giving me notes that weren't related to the story and I was miserable. And then, ultimately when they passed on it, they said "This is too smart."

So I got depressed. And then I said, "You want stupid? I'll show you fucking stupid like you've never seen." Now ultimately that isn't what I did, but it was a reaction.

I wound up going into Fox and they said writers keep coming in wanting to do movies about nerds, but that they wanted something about the in crowd. I said, "Okay, if I can make them idiots." And they said, "We don't care – we just want something about the in crowd."

And then I thought, I want to do something about a really, really happy person. Someone who is the opposite of what I am. So I made this girl where if you yell at her, she just thinks it's silly and she never gets hurt. And she's always happy, no matter what's happening. And then I thought, I wonder where she would fit? And then I remembered (Jane Austen's) *Emma* and I re-read *Emma*. And I did a pilot and they said, "Nah."

So I got a new agent and he read it and said, "This should be a movie." And so he sold it as a movie.

How had you changed as a director between *Fast Times* and *Clueless*?

That's so hard to say, because you're not the same person on any level. The only thing I can tell you with assurance is how my face has changed.

NANCY SAVOCA ON "TRUE LOVE"

How did you get interested in filmmaking?

NANCY: My family says I started talking about it when I was really young, but I don't remember that. But I think it was in high school, during that last year when you can take whatever you want. I was taking things like Folk Poetry and Music Theory. And there was a History of the Movies class. That was the first time I understood what a director did. It was explained that there was actually one person who was in charge of putting all the different elements together in a film.

And that was something that was really interesting, because I think in my teenage years I was really interested in the arts -- I loved music and I loved drawing and I loved watching actors perform. There were so many things that I loved, yet I didn't feel that I was particularly good at these things. But I was a great appreciator of good music and good performance and good photography -- I could appreciate it.

So I realized, when I learned about filmmaking, that that's what a director does. They are the ones who say, "Oh, that's the piece of music we need to use," and "That's the take we need to print." Basically, we're there to cheerlead all these great artists and get their best work and put it all together.

When I found out that's what it was, I was like, "Oh, sign me up! That sounds good. I can do that." I was about seventeen at the time.

So how did you make that happen?

NANCY: The thought was really scary, because I didn't have a clue on how to make that happen. I just knew that it sounded really good.

I didn't come from a background that had anything -- anything! -- to do with this business. My parents -- like most parents who have a kid who'd going to do something like this -- were horrified. They were scared for me. They just wanted me to get a good job at the post office.

There was no real plan. This was my last year in high school, so I went to the teacher and asked, "Where do I learn this?" And she said, "Well, there's NYU, but that's really expensive." And I said, "No, I can't do that." And so she said, "Well, there's Queen's College."

So I started at Queen's College and I took some courses. But they were the courses that every kid who was looking to goof off would take first, so I kept getting shut out of classes. Finally I met my husband, Rich, and he was going to NYU and he said "You should go here." So he started really helping me not be so fearful about stuff. He said, "Just do this, you'll figure it out."

I was basically leaping into a void. There was no financial support, it wasn't coming from anywhere. So I just started doing it.

And at NYU I found, for the first time, a community of people who were doing the things that interested me.

I had gone to Queens College for two years, so when I went to NYU I was in my final two years, and film was all I did there. All I did was shoot.

In order to enter the school, Haig Manoogian, who was running the program at that point, told me I needed to take this course called Sight and Sound. It was six of weeks of, I call it Basic Training, where you ate, slept, breathed, whatever, film. And you really couldn't do anything else, because that's all you had time to do.

The odd thing for me was that a week before I started that six weeks of basic training I got married. So here I am, this newlywed, having made a commitment to this person, and suddenly I was missing.

So Rich came looking for me and realized that I was having a really good time. As insane as it was, it was pretty amazing.

He was going to NYU for business. He used to show up just to help lug equipment around, but then he quickly realized that we were all flakey people and needed some kind of organization, which he was able to do. So he ended up doing things like production managing on student films, like mine in particular. Which was when we first started working together, which was really good. We just celebrated 28 years. But if we hadn't worked together, I don't think there's any way we could have survived, because we were coming from such different places.

We were out making our short films and the missing element always -- always! -- was how to manage time, so that we could get things done on time. No one really was teaching us that. We had a lot of enthusiasm and ideas, but we didn't have a lot of discipline. And Rich came along and he's very good at that. He'd say things like, "You know, if you shoot this first, you can actually do this all in one day if you switch the order of your locations." He actually should have been given credit as being one of our teachers, but he was our age.

How many people were in the class?

NANCY: Maybe twenty-five, twenty-eight people.

And how many were women?

NANCY: About four or five.

Talking about women in film, one of things that was sort of a blow to me, I was sitting in class one day with a teacher I really respected a lot. We were chatting about the great directors and the work they did and out of the blue (or, at least, it felt out of the blue), he said something like, "So the reason there are no women directors is that, basically, they get married and have kids."

And I had gotten married a couple of weeks earlier. And when I made *True Love*, I had an 18-month old baby and was pregnant with my second child, so they do get married and have kids. Maybe.

As a pregnant director, did you have trouble getting insurance for the production?

NANCY: Yes we did. When we started *Household Saints*, Jonathan Demme was our executive producer and I think they had tried to make him the back-up director if anything happened to me. But they couldn't because at that time I wasn't union and he was DGA, so Rich was the back-up director. And all Rich kept saying to me was, "Don't fuck anything up. I don't want to be directing."

Let's back-up. What did you do when you got out of NYU?

NANCY: Right after film school was finished, we started writing *True Love*, that summer. I remember one of the things that sort of upset me were rules. Like people had these ideas, these rules. Like one person said to me that summer, "It's great that you're writing your first feature, but you usually have to direct two shorts to do a feature." And then somebody else said, "No, no, no, So-and-So just went out to LA. You have to get an agent and write two screenplays for other people, and then you get to direct your first feature."

And I thought, "Who made those rules? I've never heard of directors who follow these rules. Is someone making up new ones just so we can jump through hoops? This is stupid."

So Rich and I co-wrote *True Love* in a couple weeks in a cabin in Vermont, which was so bizarre because we were writing about the Bronx and we were in the middle of nowhere in Vermont.

When we came out with it, basically nothing happened. We were showing it around; we didn't know. I didn't even have, at that time, the vocabulary to say this is an independent film or not an independent film. I just wanted to make this story because I hadn't seen it before. It was the old 'write what you know,' so I wrote what I knew, which was my experience, which happened to be right before we started film school: Which was that I got married, and that year that I got married, everybody in my neighborhood got married. So we went to a lot of weddings and witnessed a lot of the things that ended up in the script.

Basically it was just Rich and I writing down everything that we knew. We sent it out -- cable television was just starting up -- and we got the rejection letters. We were nobody, as they say in the Bronx.

So basically it was six years of trying this, that and the other thing. About every six to eight months we'd take the script out and polish it up. But for whatever reason, there was just nothing else I could think to do. I just knew that this was the story. Whether that was smart or not, I can't tell you. But it was six years.

During those six years we started working in film, in any capacity that we could. I started off as a production assistant for John Sayles and Maggie Renzi on *Brother From Another Planet* -- that was the first official film job I got after I got out of school.

For being the first person in my family -- and, for a long time, the only person in my family -- to get a college degree, I got to work for free on a movie. I think after I'd been there a couple weeks, they gave all of us who were volunteering a raise and we got five dollars a week, so we could take the subway to work, so we weren't actually out of pocket to work on the movie.

From there, what was fantastic -- and I say this to everybody who's looking to work in film -- do put yourself out there and just work on productions. Because that's where you're going to meet people. And sure enough, there's a very direct connection between the first job I ever had and my first film, which is John Sayles, who was one of our investors six years later.

Everybody's story is so different. Sometimes I hesitate, when we're in front of students or something, I say, "I'm going to tell you my story and you're going to think, 'Yeah, right, that will never happen to me.' And that's true, but you're going to have a different story."

But what does happen is that when you open yourself up and you let every single person on the planet know that you want to do this, and that you're going to do this, people start coming around out of curiosity or the people who are going to be drawn to you will start coming toward you because you're letting everyone know that you're ready to do this. And that's what I think started happening.

But it took six years, and nobody likes to hear that. But in that time we honed our skills and we learned a lot about production so that by the time we made our movie, we had been on a lot of sets and worked in different capacities. I was a Production Coordinator, I was an Assistant Editor, for John Sayles I was at one point a Storyboard Artist, which was really fun because it was for Bruce Springsteen and I was such a fan.

So what was it that finally got *True Love* off the ground?

NANCY: John Sayles.

What happened was I was sort of half-ass shooting this documentary that wasn't working. And one of my friends said, "What are you doing shooting a documentary? You have this script." And I said, "Yeah, but I need money to shoot that script and we don't have money." But it put this idea in my head and we decided to take what tiny little money we had to do the documentary and take that money -- which was basically all the savings we had at that time -- and do a ten-minute sample reel, which is sort of like a long version of a trailer.

So we put an ad in *Backstage* and did casting, found a crew that was mostly commercial people or people who had worked in independent films and were working a step below and wanted to step up. And since everyone was working at one level higher than normal, nobody needed to get paid, which was great, because everybody was doing it for <u>their</u> reel.

We shot over the course of a couple weekends, because everybody had day jobs. and then we thought, we should send this out instead of the script, because what we didn't know -- and I'm a Leo, so I think I'm great -- what we didn't know from my student films that did get good responses from people, that I could direct and I could grab an audience. And the script never shows that. It's like the difference between a map of Paris and Paris -- how can you explain? When you're writing a screenplay, you're basically being the best mapmaker you can be. But it's such a different animal to putting it on the screen.

So I knew by at least giving them a taste of what I could do with it, this material, that I could get more support.

So we shot this thing, we cut it, it looked great, the performances were great -- we got these great actors -- and we started sending it to all the people who had rejected the script, and we were universally rejected again. After spending all the money we had.

We were just depressed. And then we decided to do a screening in Manhattan and -- because, during those six years of working -- we had met so many people in the film business. So we just cast the net really wide and we invited everybody that we knew to invite everybody that they knew.

We had wine and cheese and ten minutes is painless. I don't know why, but people showed up. Diane Keaton showed up. I don't know why. But because it was New York and it was such a little closed community, for some reason, people showed up.

What happened after that was that I got a phone call from John Sayles and he said, "Look, if you want to do this movie down and dirty, guerilla style, I'll be your first investor."

We had also in those six years worked with Jonathan Demme. Kenny Utt, who was Jonathan's producer, said, "I'm going to be an investor." And he turned to Jonathan and said, "You better be an investor." And then Susan Seidelman was an investor. And so all of a sudden, something caught fire and I can't tell you what it is, and that's why when I tell this story people always roll their eyes and say, "That will never happen to me." No, it won't happen to you -- another story will happen to you.

But it can be that crazy.

So then we got all these -- we like to call them -- celebrity investors, and with a handful of celebrity investors we still needed more money, but these were names that we could use when we went to our friend who's mother's dentist wanted to invest in film. And he got to be an investor along with all these really great filmmakers.

So how did you feel on the first day of shooting *True Love*?

NANCY: Great. Nervous as hell. Ready to puke -- I couldn't tell if it was morning sickness. But nobody knew I was pregnant. Nobody knew because I found out two weeks before we started shooting and the one thing you don't want to tell everybody who'd investing in you on your first film is, "Oh, by the way, I'm pregnant."

I think today it might be a little easier. Or maybe not. Who knows. But I definitely knew to keep my mouth shut.

I was nervous on one level but also just like -- excited, but relieved. It was like, "Okay. Well here I am. Let's go." And it was that leap into the void of "Let's go. I don't know what's going to happen here, but I'm here. You're here. Let's go."

How did you find your cast?

NANCY: I knew exactly what I was looking for, and it was very difficult to find, interestingly enough for two reasons. One was that we didn't have the budget to go through the Screen Actors Guild. We couldn't afford to work with any sort of union, so most of the actors we were looking at were young actors who were somewhat inexperienced, but the ones who were really good had a theater background. Which was great and actually very helpful, because coincidentally they were coming in with the same background I had, which was theater acting classes.

The issue was finding experienced actors, and the problem was bigger with the older actors, because finding non-SAG actors of that age was very tricky. So we kept casting from the time that we did

the ten-minute trailer until two years later, when we started shooting. We were always looking for actors. People used to make fun of
me, saying, "Oh, you're still casting?"

With Annabella we were incredibly lucky, because she was one of
the first people we saw from the Backstage ad we placed for the
trailer. I saw her picture and said, "I hope she's good because she is
right, she is who I'm looking for." And she walked in and read it and
I thought, "Did she begin? Did someone tell her to start performing
or is she just talking to me?" She was amazing. that started a relationship that lasted through the years and she was able to be in the
film.

So she was around for two years and Ron Eldard we found I think
two weeks before we started shooting. It was horrible. We could not
find this guy.

And what was very interesting in *True Love*, because we weren't
using SAG actors, all the actors we worked with -- with the excep-
tion of Annabella, who had done a TV movie -- no one had ever
been in front of a camera before. And that's a big cast -- I forget how
many people were in that movie, but it was a lot of people.

And just about every other day -- sometimes it was every day --
we'd have a new actor working, and I kept wondering why things
were taking so long. And then I remembered: "Oh, yeah, they've
never been in front of a camera before!" And I'd have to go tell them,
"You can walk from here to here, don't walk off camera, there's a
light stand, don't do this, now deliver the line to his left shoulder." It
was really about making people feel very comfortable so they could
look like they weren't acting.

It's all about making them comfortable. Your job, especially if they're
less experienced, they have to feel really good to let go and take a
risk in their performance.

Tell me about your experience at Sundance with *True Love*.

NANCY: It was pretty amazing but I wasn't there. I wasn't even
there.

We finished editing the movie in late 1988. John Sayles said there
was a festival we should look into, called the United States Film
Festival in Park City. We did a temp mix on the soundtrack and sent
it in and we go accepted.

The festival was the last week of January and my due date was the 27th of January, so I wasn't going to go. So one of the producers went, with my lawyer and the music supervisor.

I was at home and I started going into labor one evening. And the phone rings while I'm in labor. My husband picks it up and then he says, "Oh my God. Oh my God. I'll put Nancy on, but I'm not sure she can breath."

So I take the phone and say, "What?" And everyone was screaming. It sounded like Beatlemania or something. Everyone was screaming. And someone was saying, "We won! We won!" And I said, "What?" And they said, "The film won!"

But I really didn't understand what had happened, because nobody could talk really, and also because I was hugging the wall and breathing. And so I said, "I have to hang up because this kid's going to be born." I hung up the phone and we went to the hospital.

The next morning the baby was born. And the midwife said to me, "What happened to that little movie you were working on when you were pregnant?" And I turned to Rich and said, "Did we win something last night?"

We came home with my son a day later, and my house looked like a funeral. Everybody sent flowers. It was a small apartment and there were flowers everywhere. Disney sent a t-shirt for the baby that said, "My Mom is the world's greatest director." Every single major studio was acknowledging the award and the baby.

I was flabbergasted because independent film, before that night, at Sundance, a new wave began for independent film. It was born in a different way that night. I didn't happen to be there, but I was a part of it.

And that particular year, they changed the name from the US Film Festival to the Sundance Film Festival. I have a poster that says "*True Love*: Winner of the United States Film Festival," because MGM didn't realize that they had changed the name.

And that was the year that all the studio executives showed up. There had been rumblings; the year before a lot of great movies were there and they were saying, "Oh, I guess something's happening at Sundance, so we have to go."

And that was the year that they all went.

SUSAN SEIDELMAN ON "DESPERATELY SEEKING SUSAN"

How did you get started in filmmaking?

SUSAN: When I started out, I thought I wanted to be a fashion designer. When I originally went to college, I went to a school in Philadelphia for design. Just on a whim I took a film appreciation course; this was in the mid-70s, and film schools were not nearly as popular as they are today. I liked watching movies and I got hooked on watching movies.

And then I kept taking more and more film appreciation classes. They didn't have film equipment, and it was certainly before digital, so it wasn't like you could take your home video camera and make a movie. So I started to make radio plays, because they had a radio studio at the school.

Little by little I realized that one of the things that I liked about film was that it combined a lot of the things I was interested in, like design, storytelling, music. And then on a whim I decided to apply to NYU film school. It was not that hard to get into film school back then, and so without ever having made a film (I sent them a design portfolio with the radio drama tapes I'd made), somehow I got accepted.

But once I started film school and got the chance to make my own little films and work on crews and play with the equipment, I realized that was not only something that I loved, but it was something that I found I was kind of good at, on the student level. I was nominated for a student Academy Award, so I was getting positive feedback from the little student films I was making and I was able to win some grants to continue to make longer and longer short films.

But I never really thought how I was going to have a career as a filmmaker. I wasn't very pragmatic in terms of having a long-term plan; I just was making these little films and they were winning some awards and I was getting money to make a longer film. So basically what happened was, after I graduated from film school, I stayed in touch with the people who I had worked with in film school. As my films were getting longer (from a twenty-minute film to a thirty-minute film to my last short film, which was forty-five-minutes), I figured, why not try to make an eighty or ninety-minute film?

So, using the same crew I had been working with earlier, we just did that. I don't even know how. It was just very naive; it was kind of like one of those Judy Garland/Mickey Rooney musicals: 'Hey, let's put on a show!'

My grandmother had passed away and I had a little bit of money, about $20,000. So I was going to make a feature film for $20,000. All the people who worked on it did it for a little bit of rent money and some food and deferred salaries that they thought they would never get. But that film turned out to be *Smithereens*, which was invited to the Cannes Film Festival, and that put me on a professional path.

But I never really planned it and I certainly didn't have any role models to speak of. I had heard of Ida Lupino but I didn't really know of her films. The only role models I did have were some European women, like Agnes Varda and Lina Wertmüller.

But in terms of American women, every once in a while I'd hear about one woman who made a film, but they were more one-off kind of things. But except for Ida Lupino and Dorthy Arzner from the very early days, I didn't know of any women who had a career as a film director and a body of work.

So instead of planning it, with one thing leading into the next, I sort of stumbled into making this feature film that got some attention and got picked up for distribution by New Line Cinema. It made some money and I was able to pay back the deferments to the cast and crew, who had never expected to make any money from this. The film got some good reviews and the next thing I knew I had an agent in Los Angeles who was sending me some scripts.

It sounds like your transition from making shorts to making a feature was pretty seamless and painless.

SUSAN: It really was, because the short films just kept getting longer. And I realized, after the forty-five-minute short, that it just seemed stupid to do a sixty-minute short; I just figured, why not make it eighty or whatever. And that became a feature.

Today young filmmakers are very savvy. They know how to get an agent, what's going on at the box office at any given moment. But back then it was pre-Internet and on TV there was no *Entertainment Tonight,* so people didn't really know -- or at least, I didn't really know -- that much about the business. And to some extent that was a blessing, because my efforts were totally uncalculated. I never thought, 'I'm going to make this film to get an agent.' I just made the film because it was a story I wanted to tell.

I never thought about how to get a distributor. My ignorance was, in a way, an asset, because I was just doing it for the passion of wanting to make this movie. Which is the best way to do it.

One of the problems I notice now, teaching at a pretty high-profile film school, is that the kids, because they are not naive, are already calculating to some extent how to make the movie that's going to get them the agent. Or what did what at the box office. Or this kind of movie does well and if I get this actor than I can do this. As opposed to just focusing on this is a story that I really want to tell and I think I'm going to tell it in a unique way.

How did you make the often treacherous transition from self-generating your material to looking at scripts submitted by studios?

SUSAN: *Smithereens* went to the Cannes Film Festival in 1982. There were a few women who had made a one-off movie that had gotten some attention and then they made their next movie, a studio movie, that didn't work and then I never heard of them again. So I was aware of the fact that if your first movie is the movie you've been waiting your whole life to make, and you're doing it your way, that you want to make sure that the next movie you make -- when you suddenly have people looking over your shoulder and you have an outside producer who isn't your best friend from film school -- that you better make the right choices. Because it's so easy to get overwhelmed by the process. You better choose your material wisely.

So between 1982 and 1984 I had this agent and I was getting sent some scripts; a lot of them were dumb and some of them were things I just couldn't relate to. And then I read this script called *Desperately Seeking Susan* and it just spoke to me.

The subject matter was a little bit about a world I knew, because it was set in downtown New York and that's where *Smithereens* was set. But it also had a bigger component, because it combined two worlds: it had this suburban housewife character and it had this downtown street character that was very similar to the kind of world I had dealt with in *Smithereens*.

So it felt like the right organic step -- like going from longer shorts to a feature -- and I wasn't going far outside of the world I was interested in, but yet it was expanding that world a little bit. It was telling a more complicated story and it was a bigger budget, but it wasn't such a big budget that I didn't think I could handle it.

And the other interesting thing about it was that the two producers who had sent me the script -- Midge Sanford and Sarah Pillsbury -- were first-time producers. So it was like I was the experienced one, because I had made a low-budget feature already. So I didn't feel like I was getting this big, heavy Hollywood producer looking over my shoulder who was going to intimidate me. It was two women that I liked and for who it was their first time, too.

Can you remember any of the scripts you were sent that you said "no" to?

SUSAN: I remember one script that I was sent that I think got made into a movie. I think a woman ended up directing and it's a movie that you probably would never remember. I think it was called *The Joy of Sex*. It was like a book title that they tried to turn into a movie but didn't. It didn't take off.

As a female director, the kinds of things I was sent were teen girl movies. There's nothing wrong with teen girl movies if they're interesting -- certainly Amy Heckerling did a very interesting one, *Fast Times at Ridgemont High* -- but the one I was getting sent weren't that good.

How involved were you in the casting of *Desperately Seeking Susan*?

SUSAN: I was pretty involved in the casting, but I wasn't involved in Rosanna Arquette. When Midge and Sarah brought me the script, Rosanna was already attached. She was a given.

It took some time to get the movie financed, so we worked together on script revisions and meetings at studios trying to get it made for several months.

When we knew that the film was going to be green lit, at Orion, it was due to a woman who was in a senior position at Orion Pictures, Barbara Boyle. When she green lit the project, with Mike Medavoy, we started the casting.

We had a casting office here in New York and because I'm a New Yorker I was somewhat familiar with the New York talent pool. I had heard of Madonna -- she actually lived a couple blocks from me in downtown Manhattan -- her career hadn't quite taken off yet, she had one single out that was getting some attention. So I knew of her as the up-and-coming singer who was a downtown New York personality.

Did you face any resistance to casting her?

SUSAN: No, because I was the one that brought them Madonna, they didn't bring me Madonna. They were the ones saying, 'I don't know if we can go with this person because I've never heard of her.' And I was the one saying, 'I think she's right for this character. Let me do a screen test.' And she was right for the character.

Did you feel intimidated at all once it became a studio picture?

SUSAN: No so much, because I really felt that this was the right movie for me. I've made movies that I'd say probably weren't the best movie for me. But in this film I just knew that world. I waited until I got the right subject matter. I grew up in the suburbs; I was a suburban girl. I could have been the Rosanna Arquette character. I had chosen to move to New York and live a different kind of life and so I related to the Madonna character. So for me it was the perfect blend of these two worlds I knew and I had a unique way of wanting to tell this story. And I think when you feel that you're in control of your vision, people can't really intimidate you that much, because it's your vision.

Somebody else could have made the film differently, but I felt like I knew how to make that version of the film.

There are probably many movies that I couldn't have made and I probably would have felt intimidated trying to direct because I was crossing into territory that other people might have been able to do much better or had done better. But because I think this movie was the right one for me, and I think because it was also characters that I knew and a studio executive couldn't tell be how to direct that character better, it gave me a certain amount of confidence.

Of course, technically, I had never worked with that size of a crew and those kinds of gaffers and grips and lighting and all that. But it was a fortuitous experience. I was surrounded by people who were artistically simpatico. I had supportive producers, Midge and Sarah who weren't heavy-handed. And I had a great DP, Ed Lachman, who was a New Yorker who had also come from an independent, European style of cinematography. He wasn't like a heavy, union guy. So we worked really well together; the way we thought about cinema was simpatico.

And the other department heads were first-timers. Like Santo Loquasto, who was the production designer and costume designer, had worked as a costume designer on Woody Allen's films, but this was the first time he was going to be doing both.

It was a wonderful growing experience for a lot of people. The casting directors had cast theater stuff, but this was their first film.

What did you learn doing *Desperately Seeking Susan* that you were able to take to future projects?

SUSAN: Learning how to work with a crew. One of the things I realized is that it's a collaborative art form, so you're dealing with so many different people, all of whom have their own artistic vision. The director's job is to maintain a single, artistic vision by coordinating everyone else's. Everyone wants to give as much as they can, but it can become a real hodgepodge if there's not one, unifying way of looking at the film -- one unifying vision.

I watched movies where I felt that things were out of control because all the actors were doing something different and all trying to do something to the max and it really needed someone to say, 'No, don't do that. Yes, do that.' Learning how to modulate things, whether it's the performances or learning when to be flashy with the camera and when to be subtle. When to not move the camera and when to move it.

It's all about trying to maintain this one vision and that's what I started to see in *Desperately Seeking Susan*. I'm still learning, it's an ongoing process. But that's the skill that I realized that good directors have, being able to get what they need and incorporate other people's ideas; knowing how to use the best and politely (without hurting people's feelings) not use the stuff that you don't think works.

Sometimes different directors find different ways of doing that. I've heard about or seen examples of male directors who seem to feel that they have to be like drill sergeants and Nazis to show that they're the boss. Scream and get into fistfights and do that macho tough thing.

Now, as a woman, that isn't a style that particularly works for me, and as a woman who's just a little over five feet, I knew that no one was going to be physically intimidated by me. So I had to find my own way and have found my own way over the years of getting what I needed in a different way.

As I get older, I change the way I get what I need. But certainly, for me, it had to be different than my impression of what a typical, Erich Von Stroheim or John Ford kind of macho male director is like on the set.

Do you think that some scripts were never sent to you, just because you're a woman?

SUSAN: I don't know. The fact of the matter is, there aren't tons of great scripts out there. I think all directors, men and women, will say the same thing. There's not a lot of great scripts out there. You've really got to struggle to find the good ones. And sometimes you do the good ones, and sometimes you do the ones you hope will be good -- they're kind of okay and you hope you can turn it into something fantastic. Sometimes it works and sometimes it doesn't.

Do you think it's easier for women today than when you started back with *Smithereens*?

SUSAN: Honestly, I don't. I want to be encouraging, but I want to be honest, too.

There are opportunities, but I think the opportunities are in new media. I think that, right now, the movie industry is going through a major change. The studios are all owned by huge, multi-national corporations. There are fewer studios. A lot of the studios from fifteen or even ten years ago have been gobbled up and turned into one big corporate thing. There's no longer a New Line, there's no longer an Orion, there's no longer a Tri-Star, there's no longer a Warner Independent. There are just a lot of companies that don't exist anymore. The big studios are making fewer movies, but they're trying to make movies that are bigger budgeted and have the potential to make hundreds of millions of dollars, not just a hundred million.

But where there are more opportunities, I think, is in the independent sector, but in that case it's women making their own opportunities. They're writing their own script, and then they're trying to get a cast attached, and then they're trying to go out and find the financing.

So what still excites you about making movies?

SUSAN: Telling stories, that's what excites me. Telling stories. And that's what excited me in the beginning. To me, characters and stories are the heart of what makes a movie great. And although I'm always impressed when I see movies that have amazing technology and amazing special effects, it's the more human aspect of it that really grabs me.

LESLI LINKA GLATTER ON "TWIN PEAKS," "THE WEST WING" AND MORE ...

You didn't start out with a strong desire to be a filmmaker, right?

LESLI: No. But I was always a storyteller, just in a different medium. I've always wanted to tell stories and communicate in some sort of deep way, but it wasn't in film. That came later.

How did you start out as a dancer and then become a director?

LESLI: I'm always fascinated by everyone's story and how they got into film, because no one seems to have the same story.

I was a modern dance choreographer -- I was a dancer and then a choreographer. Back when the American government actually sponsored the arts -- which is so long ago that most people who remember it are rolling on their walkers or breathing on oxygen -- I was sent to Asia to teach and choreograph and perform throughout the Far East.

I had spent five years in Europe -- in Paris and in London -- and I based out of New York. The I got this grant and went to Asia, studying classical Japanese theater and dance and teaching modern dance.

By chance, in a coffee shop, I met an older man who was in his late seventies when I first met him, and he became like my mentor or my Japanese father. I met him completely by chance -- which is one of the themes I keep getting pulled to in terms of storytelling -- and he turned out to be head of cultural affairs for the country. He spoke twelve languages, had been a Buddhist monk, had been the top foreign war correspondent, just an amazing man.

Eventually he told me a series of six stories. What they had in common was that they all happened on different Christmas Eves (even though he was Buddhist and not Christian), all during different wars, and all about human connection. When he told me these stories, I knew I had to pass them on and I knew it wasn't dance.

If I hadn't have met this old, Japanese guy in a coffee shop in Tokyo, I would never have become a film director.

You weren't kidding when you used the phrase, "by chance."

LESLI: Of course, I didn't immediately go out and direct. I thought, "Well, maybe it's a theater piece," because I had directed theater. Then I ended up meeting a filmmaker in Japan, named George Miller, who directed *Road Warrior*. Other than Australia, Japan was one of the first places that released *Road Warrior*. So if you were living in Japan, at that time, if you were a Westerner, you kind of ran into most of the Westerners around at some point.

I told George about my story and he said, "I think you have a film here." And I though, "Hmm, that's interesting."

Eventually I moved back to America and I ended up in Los Angeles. I was on the faculty of the California Institute of the Arts and these stories kept haunting me. Then I met someone who told me about the directing workshop for women at the American Film Institute (AFI), so I applied to that program. I got the application and realized that I was totally unqualified. It was set up for women in the film business who hadn't directed.

Well, I wasn't in the film business, I didn't know anybody in the film business. But I thought, "You know what? I'm going to apply anyway. The worst-case scenario is that it makes me put my ideas down on paper and make it really clear for me."

So I did that and I got in. That year they let in a couple of women who were not film makers -- one theater director and myself as a choreographer.

What was your next step after your AFI experience?

LESLI: I had a very fortuitous situation. You make these little films for no money. And I didn't have parents who have money. I had no connections to the film business, so it wasn't like I could look to family and say, "Look, I need to make a film, could you help me out here?" I've always had to work to make a living. And I say that only because there are people who definitely don't have to. I've been surprised at how many people there are.

We'd sent the film off to all these festivals and to be considered for an Academy Award, which was like a dream you couldn't even imagine. But it actually got nominated. Even now I don't know how that happened. But it was one of three films that got nominated in the short film category. So all of a sudden I'm getting calls from agents.

How did that feel?

LESLI: It was wild! It felt very surrealistic.

Actually, the very first job I did after my short film, my first professional job, was for a TV series that Steven Spielberg had, called Amazing Stories. That was like my film school. It was an extraordinary opportunity and he was beyond generous. I apprenticed with him and with Clint Eastwood. I followed him around on a couple of projects and it really taught me a lot about the process.

So you were learning on Steven Spielberg's set?

LESLI: Yes. At AFI I had worked on about ten of the other women's films before I directed my own short film, because I didn't come from a film background I felt that I needed to understand what the process was. I mean, I looked at credits when I first started directing and I didn't know what a Key Grip did. I didn't know anything about film. So I did any job I could on the other women's films before I directed my film. I was the last one to shoot. And I very purposefully did that. Again, I think it comes from being a dancer, where you just can't cheat. So I felt like I needed to understand what the process was, as much as I could being a beginner.

When your film is nominated, you're kind of out there for that brief little period. You're an asparagus and it's asparagus season, but you know pretty soon it's going to be carrot season and nobody will want to hear about asparaguses anymore. That's just the reality.

But during that time I got a call from Spielberg and I thought it was one of my friends playing a joke. So I hung up. Thank goodness he called me back. So I went in and met with him. He said he was starting this show, *Amazing Stories*, and he asked if I wanted to direct one. And I was like, "Oh my God, of course, yes. That would be incredible. But I would like to apprentice with you before I do it." So that's what I did. And it was the best film school I could have imagined.

I did my first episode (I ended up doing three of them), which was my first day of shooting on a professional set.

What did you shoot the first day?

LESLI: It was two hundred guys, in World War II, storming a beach in Italy. I think I had nine cameras and three Eyemos. That was my first day on a professional set.

How did you feel?

LESLI: I was terrified. I had a dream a couple of nights before, a stress dream, that you can't even imagine. It was one of those horrible things: You walk on the set and it's a crew you don't know and they're shooting a film you've never read, and the set was floor to ceiling pea-green sofas. It had nothing to do with the story I'd prepped. I was totally panicked.

I told Steven about it and he said, "You know, I have a dream like that before I start everything." And I thought, "Wow. Here's one of the great filmmakers of our time who's saying he has that fear too." He was great at saying and doing things like that.

Anyway, it was terrifying. All I could do to make myself feel better was to be as prepared as I could be. That's how I felt comfortable, because I felt I could do it by knowing what I wanted -- by having seen the film in my head. In the beginning, that was my security blanket.

So you made it through Amazing Stories. What happened next?

LESLI: The next big step for me, in terms of creative process, was working on David Lynch's TV series, *Twin Peaks*. I directed four episodes and that was another huge turning point for me.

There was a scene in the pilot for the show in which Michael Ontkean is talking to Kyle Macachlan. It's in a bank, in a room where you look at your safety deposit box. In the middle of the scene, on this table, is this moose head. They play the whole scene in this room and no one ever refers to the moose head. The scene is incredible.

So, when I got to know David, I went up to him and said, "How did you ever get the idea to put the moose head on the table?" He looked at me like I was kind of crazy, and he said, "It was there." And I said, "What do you mean it was there?" He said, "The set decorator was going to hang it on the wall," and David said to the decorator, "Leave the moose head."

Something just cracked open in my brain: "Be sure you're open to the moment. Be sure you see the moose head on the table. Don't try to control things so much that you're not open to what's happening in the moment."

That was a great lesson and a huge turning point for me.

From Steven I learned, "Do your homework and never pretend you know what you don't, because someone is going to be there who knows and you're going to get caught." Which was all about planning and control.

And from David I learned, "Yes, do all of that, but be sure you're open to the moment."

I have definitely had difficult people to deal with, people that I wouldn't work with again. But more often than not I've had really good experiences.

I think in general the crew wants you to be good. I don't think that they want you to be bad. I think they want to know that you're someone who has done their homework. As a director, we can't do it without the whole crew. It's a team sport. We need everyone.

I think when you go on the set, I don't think a crew immediately respects a guy just because he's a guy or disrespects a woman because she's a woman. I think they want some to know what they're doing. If you do, they'll be great. And if you're nice, they'll even be better.

If you do simple things, like at night go to the truck and thank everybody. Just common, human traits. I think if you treat people with respect and challenge them to do great work and thank them for the work that they do, they're going to be really great.

Have I met people who are really difficult and undermining? Absolutely. Absolutely. But I think part of the job is figuring out how to deal with them.

I tried to narrow down just one of the shows you've worked on. And since I'm such an Aaron Sorkin fan --

LESLI: Oh my God, so am I.

Then I hope you'll indulge me and talk about your experiences on both *The West Wing* and *Studio 60*.

LESLI: I think the reason *The West Wing* was amazing to do, on a directorial level, was because the producing director on the show -- Tommy Schlamme, a fantastic director and a wonderful person -- encouraged directors to come in and make it their movie.

There are many people who work in TV who want it to look like everybody else's show. But I really think the best shows do what Tommy did. To say to filmmakers, "Come in and make it your movie." And that's what he did.

That's very evident on that show. They're all different.

LESLI: They're all different. As a director, you were encouraged to do what you wanted to do. If you wanted to put five scenes together and do it as one shot, you could. It was great.

It was very intimidating the first time I got Aaron's script and I looked at the first scene I was going to be directing on my first day. It was a seven-page scene, with about ten or eleven characters, and the only stage direction was "He enters."

I just thought, "Oh my God." I had to read it about ten times to figure out what the scene was about: What's the subtext, what's the text, what's really going on underneath here.

It was thrilling and terrifying and exhilarating and amazing.

https://www.youtube.com/watch?v=HMn2s1nmsxQ

What is your preparation process like in a case like that? You get the script and then what?

LESLI: The first thing I do in any prep process is I start breaking the script down in terms of what is the theme? What is this really about? Once I figure out the theme, I start to figure out how I'm going to deal with it visually. But until I really know what it's about in a deep way, I can't even begin to figure that out.

How long does that take?

LESLI: That's ongoing. The first couple of days I focus on the script as much as I can. You're going to have to deal with production stuff no matter what. You have to start the casting process and have a concept meeting about if there have to be huge sets built. A lot of *The West Wing* episodes I did were really big, so there were tons of locations, so there was a lot of scouting. Plus, half of the show shoots in Washington, DC, so there were all sorts of production issues and decisions.

Usually what I would do in terms of actual shot lists is that I would come in on the weekend. And I still do that, even though I'd love to have my weekends to myself. I find that during the week, with a TV pre-production schedule, I don't have time to do that. So, the weekends are my creative time.

If it takes place on a set, I'll go to the set. I'll walk around, I'll imagine the scene, I'll figure out the angles, I'll see the scene.

In the case of *The West Wing*, how much rehearsal time did you get with the actors?

LESLI: You only get it on the set. That was a show where they would rehearse a lot. This is unusual in TV. You'd get probably an hour. That is considered a long rehearsal. It's not like doing a film.

But then, these actors know the characters. So, you have to direct them in the scene, but they're not figuring out who their characters are. They're figuring what their behavior is. So that is a different process.

During post, how involved were you in the editing?

LESLI: Very involved. You have a certain amount of time, per the contract with the Directors Guild, to go in and edit. I didn't have my cuts changed very much. Ultimately, the final cut is Aaron's and Tommy's. When the buck stopped, it stopped with them. But they were respectful. I think they want you to come in having done it well, so that they don't have to re-do it.

This may be an ignorant question, but how do you get the show to the exact length required by the network?

LESLI: It's a bloody drag. A lot of the times, the scripts are too long. And if you have a story that's really great, some things are just going to have to go. I think it's horrible, but that's how it is. They're not going to change the time because of you, so you have to conform to what it has to be. It's really unfortunate.

At what point can you tell that you're going to be in trouble, length-wise?

LESLI: I can tell now by reading the script. I can read it and go, "Ah, this is way too long. We're going to be ten minutes over." Also, you don't have that much time to shoot.

One of the good things about directing TV is that you learn very clearly what the dollar scene is and what the five-cent scene is. You have to know what your important scene of the day is; if you're going to divide the day up, that's where you're going to want to spend the bulk of your time. And the scenes that aren't important you need to move through quickly. So, you have to find a way to shoot them that's going to tell the story. But if you have a very emotional scene that's the turning point of your story, that's where you want to be spending your time. It's not all equal. Directing TV really teaches you how to do that. Because you have to.

Let me ask about *Studio 60*, where one of the episodes you did (*Nevada Day: Part One*) was the first half of a two-part episode, where you didn't do the second half. How does that work?

LESLI: That's an interesting one. I've done that quite a bit and I've usually done it with directors that I know pretty well. I did that before with Chris Misiano on *The West Wing* as well. Chris and I know each other well and we're really good friends and connected. We talked a lot about the story together.

That was not so much the case on *Studio 60*. Scripts were coming in late and the second half of the script hadn't been written altogether. So we didn't have the luxury of that.

I knew what the ending was going to be, I knew where the story was going, it just hadn't been written yet.

What advice would you give to someone who's thinking about pursuing a directing career?

LESLI: Be sure you really want to do this. Follow your dreams. And listen -- but don't listen -- to how difficult it is. I think you have to put blinders on just proceed.

I think what's exciting about the time we're in right now is that people can pick up a camera and do it. I would advise doing that.

I think the Internet is amazing. I think the fact that you can get a camera and shoot 24p and do it for pennies with your friends -- I would say, absolutely, go for it. Go make your movie. If you want to direct, go direct.

PART II
THE EDITORS

CAROL LITTLETON ON "THE BIG CHILL"

I think the first reel of *The Big Chill* is one of the best first reels in movie history. Everything is set up so nicely.

CAROL LITTLETON: Right. All the characters are introduced.

Let me ask -- and this is just because I've always been curious about this -- William Hurt walks into the church in that reel just at the Minister is saying, ".... a man like Alex." Was that juxtaposition in the script or was it found in the editing?

CAROL LITTLETON: That was found in the editing. We could have had those entrances anywhere, in any order. Obviously he was the last one to arrive. We did cut the minister's speech down some, it was a little bit rambling. And it was just more salient to have the line over the Bill Hurt character, Nick, as he sits down.

Was that film similar to *Body Heat*, in that you found a lot of it in the editing room?

CAROL LITTLETON: It stayed closed to the script than *Body Heat*, because it was not a thriller. So we didn't have to deal with elements of timing that are alive on film but on the page are sometimes hard to judge.

But we had other things that were equally difficult, and that was how to integrate the music into the scenes and have it make sense. We discovered right away that we would not have a score, that it would be just the music from Motown stuff and things that were popular in 1968-69.

There were only two tunes that were in the script that we did to playback. For the rest of them, I cut the music and then cut the picture to the music. That was, essentially, doing it backwards. Those were not needle drops that we did after the picture was done and we just added it. It was all integrated as we were going.

I had probably 150 tunes that were in my editing room, on a rack. I would try a lot of different things until we found the right tempo and the right piece. Of course, Larry is very knowledgeable about rock and roll and that era, because he was in college then.

So most of our editorial time went into the stylistic elements of making the film. Making the music choices seem seamless and making it flow from one song to the next, so that the lyrics and the tempo and the musicality of the scene matched. Like I said, they weren't needle drops; everything was cut to the tempo of the music and re-arranged in such a way that the lyrics fell at certain moments that were salient moments in the film.

So you're kind of doing it backwards; you're literally laying the track out and putting the picture to it, rather than cutting the picture and just dropping the music in. It makes a very big difference in the flow of the film, the musicality of the film, the style of it. The style of the picture is, in fact, very musical. So those were the challenges, editorially; it was really questions of style more than anything else.

Do you have a favorite moment, where it all came together?

CAROL LITTLETON: Yes, I think the episode that was very, very difficult was with the character of Meg (Mary Kay Place) who wants to have a baby. And when Glenn Close figures out that she could put her husband with her best friend, well, it's a little preposterous. This was before artificial insemination, so if you were going to have

a baby, you actually had to have a partner. We knew that it was a little far-fetched and if the audience lost it in the movie it would probably be with that episode. The humor had to play a large part in allowing the audience to feel that it was appropriate and slightly goofy and also believable and tasteful.

So I think that whole section, with Aretha Franklin's "A Natural Woman," that whole section into the next morning, I felt really worked well for me. The night before, during the night and the next morning.

Let's talk about one of the most famous scenes in the movie -- the ending flashback, with Kevin Costner as Alex, that was shot but then cut from the movie. How did that come about?

CAROL LITTLETON: You could talk to five or six different people who worked on the movie and you'd get several different opinions. But being on the inside of that, the ending that Larry and Barbara Benedek wrote was to have a large flashback at the very end of how all these people were -- the roots of their personalities, the roots of who they were going to be -- were actually evident when they were students.

After I first read the script, we sat down and I said, "I feel very uneasy about this flashback. I just don't think you need it." And Larry with his nasal, West Virginia voice, said, "Carol, I can't believe you said that. You are so wrong. I can't believe it. You are so wrong." So I dropped it. When somebody says you're wrong, you drop it.

When we were shooting it I said, "This looks like a masquerade, with everybody in long hair and beads." And Larry said, "Carol, you are so wrong. The reason I wanted to write this script was because of this idea." And I said, "Yes, Larry, you're absolutely right. It's a wonderful idea. You may have needed that scene to write the script, but you don't need the scene for the movie. At all." "You are so wrong, if you mention this one more time!"

Well, in the editing, we put that flashback everywhere. We took it out of the ending, we put it up front, we put it in the middle, we put it in pieces, we spent a lot of time trying to get the flashback to work.

We showed it to the studio with the flashback and the suits came in -- Larry and I were the only people from our end -- and the guy who was in charge said, "This is not funny. Take it back, re-do it. I don't know what you guys are thinking, this is a comedy? This is bullshit. Start over again."

Well, we were devastated. Devastated. We knew it was funny, we knew it was engaging, we knew it was emotional.

And then he said, "While you're at it, that flashback is a stinko scene."

So we showed it to them the next time with an audience and the movie still did not work as well as it should. So I said, "Larry, why don't we devise an ending, drop the flashback, have two screenings -- one with the flashback and one without -- and let the audience tell us which one is more effective?"

Well, at the screenings, it was clear that the version without the flashback was better. And the next day, when Larry came into the cutting room, he said, "God dammit, Carol, I wanted you to take that thing out from the beginning! How many times do I have to tell you I'm right?"

That's how funny he is. He's wonderful.

DODY DORN ON "MEMENTO"

How did you get interested in film? Was editing what you always intended to do?

DODY: No. It wasn't. I grew up in LA and my father worked in the film industry. All of the female role models that I had were schoolteachers. So, I just thought, I'll be a schoolteacher. It never occurred to me that I could do something other than that.

Aside from my father, everyone else in my family was the scientist of some sort. When I got out of high school, I actually went to City College where I was taking math classes. As a product of my times, I got interested in being in the workforce and not going to school. So I started looking around for work. And it became apparent that the film industry was a place where I could get a job without a formal education.

So, I did a lot … a lot … a lot of odd jobs in film. I was in extra, I was an assistant to props, I was a production coordinator, I did some scripts supervising, I was the location manager, a lot of things.

It sounds like a great way to learn how movies are made.

DODY: Yes it was. It was great. I was the assistant to the producer and the assistant location manager on a movie of the week for Dick Clark productions call *Elvis* that was directed by John Carpenter, starring Kurt Russell.

When the film was over, they decided to make a theatrical version of the film and they brought in a different editor. The producer asked me if I was interested in staying on and working in post-production. I thought, sure. I'm curious. I'm just a curious person. So I said sure.

So I said yes to that and I self taught myself all of the things needed for being an assistant editor. From there I never looked back, because I really liked having such clearly defined skills. It was a very concrete skill set and it was marketable.

I wasn't into film as a kid, I didn't go see a million movies. But once I started working in film and seeing the alchemy, I fell in love with film and then I started to teach myself film history. Seeing classic movies. I'm still an avid classic film watcher. Most of the movies I watch are classics or art movies or foreign films.

I became fascinated by film and the magic of editing. And I took it from there.

You say you were self-taught as an assistant editor. How did you do that?

DODY: I called a friend and I said I'm getting this job as an assistant film editor, what do I need to know? And I learned over the phone the difference between the emulsion and base, how many perfs per frame, how many feet per second, etc.

I called the rental houses and learned all the names of the pieces of equipment that were used. In those days, it was a pretty straightforward mechanical process, in terms of the gear.

The job of being the assistant editor, especially in a film that has already been cut--it was a recut basically--was that of being a librarian, along with distributing the materials to the other departments that they needed for completing their parts of the recut.

I learned the names of every last single part of every piece of equipment, probably in a couple of hours. I know it sounds very mundane, but that was what I needed to know, so I learned it.

And I was very active, going and talking to all the people in all the facilities where we were working. I learned all about the lab and what was in the lab and how things were done there. I just had really good communication skills with the providers of the services. Whatever communication I could have, I did have, and learned that way.

Did you have any union issues?

DODY: No, because I got into a union on my very first job.

How did you do that? When I talked to Carol Littleton, about half of our conversation was about how tough it was for her to get into the union.

DODY: I don't even know how much of this is legitimate or not legitimate, but I was working for union company and I was gathering my days. I worked for long enough that I got my days and I went to the union and I got my checkbook out and I said, "Here are my days."

I met with the field rep at the time and I said I'm ready to sign-up. And it went from there, I signed up and I was in the union. Because I was so forthright, just standing there with my checkbook open, maybe the field rep just thought, "Ah, she's just a good kid." I don't know.

You said you self taught yourself film history. Do remember what you found to be the most useful?

DODY: There are so many great books out there about cinema, and I just went back to the early ones. Eisenstein and his theories about editing are fascinating. I was just voracious, watching and reading what I could. But that was later, by the way. The first two or three years, I was just doing my job and feeling good about having a marketable skill.

And then once I knew it inside and out, it became kind of boring, and I started to look deeper. And then I started working in sound, and when I was working sound I was examining the film in a different way. Because as an assistant film editor, you're not really examining the film. You're really more of a librarian.

Now it is easier to examine the film in its progressions. It wasn't so easy in the days of 35mm. Because you're handling the film with such kid gloves. You were just popping it up on the Movieola and watching the cut as it progressed. You, as the assistant editor, were cleaning it and repairing splices and making sure it didn't get damaged.

You weren't necessarily in dailies, you weren't necessarily in the discussions between the director and the editor. And that was the thing that kind of bummed me out. I was very appreciated as an assistant, but that is what I did. I was an assistant. I wanted to do more.

And so I went over to sound. At the time, a lot of people said, why you moving into sound? It was looked upon as a step down. For me, I am just curious by nature, I like to learn new things. So I felt I had learned as much as I could as an assistant editor, and I didn't see myself getting into the room with the film editor and learning about cutting from that.

So I became a sound assistant. And very shortly thereafter, I was cutting sound. When you're cutting sound, you see the editor's version come through and then the new version comes through and you see what's different and you begin to understand what the impact is.

My main things that I cut were dialog and Foley. And cutting Foley was very instrumental in teaching about editing because it's all about rhythms. And again, because you're watching the same material over and over and over again.

When cutting dialogue you also learn about rhythm, because you see how the cuts are made. Sometimes because they made them in the middle of the sentence. You saw which parts of which sentences could go together, and where you can make those joins. And what the impact of those things was.

So this lateral move was a very conscious choice on your part?

DODY: You know, I'm not all that sure that it was. I'm not sure that it was conscious. Mainly it was a form of appetite, more than a maneuver. I think of myself as a naïve person. In terms of politics and how to get ahead. Positioning has never been one of the things that I wanted to do. I figured I should just do what I do as well as I can. And see what happens.

But because I'm so curious, and so willing to go sideways or down or up or around, I learn a lot more.

So how did you move into the position of editor?

DODY: The same way. I was a sound editor, and then I was a supervising sound editor, and then I started a company. At some point, again, it became kind of boring, because I was doing the same thing, doing it by rote.

And then I wanted to move back into the picture department. I had been a sound editor and a supervising sound editor, by then, for 10 years. I couldn't go and be an assistant editor. So I started to look for work as an editor. And I found that I couldn't get arrested. So I went back down to the bottom, and started working for free. As a picture editor.

I worked on shorts and low budget features. I did something in Germany that was not for free, but for low pay. If it needed editing and I found it interesting, I would edit it. I was not making the salary important. That wasn't important to me. It was important that it was interesting to me.

Do you feel that you were not getting opportunities that guys were getting?

DODY: I have to say I did not perceive that, if that was true. I did hear, once in a while, someone would say, "Oh we'll hire him, he's got a wife and kids." And that would gall me. Because I did not feel that should be a criteria for filling a position. Especially a creative position.

And I have to say, I struggled quite a bit to become an editor. By struggle, I mean I worked a long time for low or no pay. And it was difficult to get into a position where I was considered.

By then, with all my work on sound, I had worked with some great directors. But those directors were not interested in giving me a shot as a picture editor. So that was frustrating, but I understand it – you need to know that someone can do what you need them to do. It's a really important position.

What was the first movie you worked on as an editor?

DODY: I did a movie called *Floundering*. Peter McCarthy directed. He was a producer. He produced *Sid and Nancy*. And that was a no pay job. After that I did an extended cut of *Terminator 2* for Jim Cameron.

And then I did *Guinevere* with Sarah Polly and Stephen Rea.

Looking back on it now, do you recommend the approach you took, the whole process of learning?

DODY: I do recommend it. I have recommended it to quite a few people. One thing about life is that it is not a thing where you just work and you arrive. It is a series of ups and downs. It's a journey. To look at the goal as an endpoint, I think can cut you off from a lot of opportunities. If that makes sense.

Have you seen the results of that advice?

DODY: One guy in particular, Matt Clark, who has cut several films for Kirby Dick. And Matt is a guy came to me with a question that most people have, maybe not expressed this naïvely. He called me up and he said, "I want you to tell me how I can get work at the Studios."

And I thought oh no. And I said, "Are you sitting down? Have you got a pencil and a piece of paper? Never ever ever ever ever call anyone ever again and ask 'How do you get a job at the studio?'"

And then I gave him my recipe. It's not really a recipe, it's my advice. And I was very forthright about it. And he followed it pretty aggressively. And he became a film editor.

One of the things that I said--and I learned this from somebody else--when I was fresh out of high school or looking for work, I had one of those very similar conversations. I was meeting somebody that I've known from my father's business. And I said, "I'm thinking of working in film."

And he said, "What do you want to do?" And I said, "Oh I'll do anything."

And he said, "Never say you'll do anything. Say you are a this or you are a that."

And that is something that I took forward and I take seriously. I am a film editor.

With Matt I said, "You want to be a film editor, do you have any money? Do you have enough money to live for a year without working? Will your parents help you out?" It was that kind of conversation.

Because what you need to do is, you need to edit. You need to edit whatever you can. You just keep editing.

I wasn't just editing anything that came along when I was working for no money. I always made sure that it was something that I would be proud to have on my resume. If at all possible.

There is one film on my resume where I noticed that the director changed the credit to an Alan Smithee film, so that must've been one where I needed to pay my rent. But for the most part, I tried to make sure that I was making my decisions based on the project and not on the money.

What project do you think you learned the most from or that provided the most challenge?

DODY: That's interesting, because I feel like I'm learning all the time. I think I'm in a state of constantly learning. I've learned on every project, so it's a hard thing for me to answer. It's like saying which one is your favorite child?

Okay, let me ask this: While you were teaching yourself film history, were there any films that really jumped out at you?

DODY: *All That Jazz* was really remarkable. Also I would say *Bonnie and Clyde* is another one. There's a kind of poetic quality to the editing that I think is really exciting. I think it also took a lot from the French New Wave.

I still see a lot of foreign films, and I see a lot of classics. I'm not, for some reason, all that interested in contemporary films.

Are you an editor or an audience member when you watch these films?

DODY: Oh, I'm an audience member. If I'm watching the technique, I feel that it is self-conscious. On the other hand, in my career when I'm reading a script, I'm always looking for scripts where the editing gets to be a character.

Like in *Memento*, the editing is a character. I did another film, *Guy*, where the editing is a character. It's a point of view film, and the point of view was a cameraperson who is a character. And so that person is a filmmaker and a cameraperson, making a documentary. And the way it is cut has to represent that person's personality.

Self-conscious editing, if it's justified, I love. Just to be self-conscious for no good reason is not interesting to me.

Requiem for a Dream was, I thought, self-conscious. I did not enjoy the self-consciousness of that. But I felt they were pushing the envelope for a reason. But it wasn't something that I responded to.

And now an example of where the self-consciousness worked for you?

DODY: Well, *All That Jazz* is a great example. The way the editor and the director together placed the sound and the image, it does grab your attention. When the sound drops out during heart attack scene, there's not a person in the theater who isn't wondering what happened? What's going on? They're suddenly conscious, and thinking that the projector is no longer making sound. At least, that's what I think happens. That's the way I felt when I was watching it.

It is certainly a wake up call. It wakes you up. You're not just rolling along.

You see, there's this funny thing about editing. It's all supposed to be invisible. And I think there is value in that. That's what the match cut is all about. But it is equally valid to have a strong hard cut that jars you, if it has a narrative purpose.

What were the special challenges you've dealt with on *Memento*?

DODY: Among the things that Chris Nolan and I talked about were, How much of the repeated material needed to be shown in order for you to understand that not only were you seeing the same thing again, but it was the exact same moment again? Because those are the clues that were laid that told you that things were going backwards. Nobody says or announces, there is no subtitle upfront, that says this is going to go backwards.

We did things with sound and music that were very identifiable. So if it was Muzak in the bathroom, it was a very identifiable piece of music. But we also use the exact same pieces of film. They weren't necessarily the same length. They were often much shorter. And we wanted it to be ever shorter and shorter throughout the course of the film.

And so we were just kind of testing that, to see how little it could be before you to recognize it. And of course once the pattern is set, then there's a rhythm about how fast we were jumping back-and-forth.

And the other funny thing about it is, that it is not really backwards. It is something that is folded in half. So you are going backwards in the color and forward in the black-and-white. And so the beginning and the end are the starting point of the story and as you are marching forward, you are getting to the middle.

And so just understanding that was fun. It was a very frustrating script to read, because you have to keep flipping pages back-and-forth and back-and-forth, because it's confusing. But that was enthralling to me.

It was fun. It was really fun. My mother was a mathematician, so I have that in me. It was kind of like a puzzle. Like I was doing my own little puzzle. And it really required a lot of intense focus, but it was very very well laid out in the script stage. We only rearranged one scene. Everything else was exactly as it was structured in the script.

What did you rearrange?

DODY: There was a point in the middle of the script where the jumping back got too frequent. So we join two sections, and dropped one repeat.

Did you do any audience testing with *Memento*?

DODY: No. We showed it to some people, but it wasn't really a test. And I think that was the right decision. It is not the kind of film where you could gather a response from the test. People always come out of that film looking like they've been hit on the back of the head with a 2 x 4. And I think that's one of the most gratifying things about it. Because the whole film is a wake up. It wakes you up.

And there are some people who are really irritated by it. And I liken that irritation to something I said to Chris in our first meeting. It reminded me of the book called *If On A Winter's Day A Traveler*.

In that book, at I think close to the end of the first chapter, some of the text is repeated. And then the author addresses the reader straight out of the page, saying "Oh, and now you've noticed that some of the text is repeated." And I thought, hey I don't want to hear this, I just want to read a story. But I wasn't the editor of that book. Reading the script of *Memento* and thinking that I might have the opportunity to be the editor of that, that was very exciting.

But as a viewer, I can understand how some people might be irritated by it. It's a matter of taste, if you want to be played with like that. Many many people just go into the theater and they want to be carried down that stream, they don't want to be woken up.

Have you had any experience with any of the films you've worked on being tested with audiences?

DODY: Yes I have.

How do you like that process?

DODY: I don't like it. Things need to be tested to be sure that audiences are following and that they understand. It depends on what kind of the film it is. So if you want people to understand, you might have to test.

I think I don't like it, because I don't like all the politics involved. It's a stressful process.

Any final advice? For someone wanting to get into the business?

DODY: The clearest advice I would give is do your best to find projects that you can believe in and work on those. And the rest may or may not follow. It's a very tricky business. And it's a tricky life. On some level, all you have is now. So you better make sure that what you're doing now is something you enjoy.

PART III
THE ACTORS

DEBRA EISENSTADT ON "OLEANNA" AND DAVID MAMET

When did you first get interested in acting?

DEBRA: I remember when I was very little being interested in plays and I used to read all the Tennessee Williams plays and all the Sam Shepard plays – all the books that my older sister had on her shelves. This was in elementary school. So I was always interested, always seeking out opportunities to be in plays. But I was never cast.

I think there are two kinds of actors. There's the writer actor and then there's the performer/singer actor. And I was always more into the writing of it. And I was always interested in writing, too. But my sister was a writer, and so I always felt like that was her territory. So I went into acting, even though I think for me I had the same feeling for writing.

Acting was very good for me for a lot of reasons, so I stayed with it. I would take the train into the city to take acting classes when I young, like fourteen. And then I majored in theater when I was in college and I went to special summer programs for acting – it was just what I did.

Then when I graduated from college, I started interning at Circle Rep, which I don't think exists anymore. It was a pretty big off-Broadway theater at one time. And then I would go on auditions through *Backstage*. And I immediately started getting work in off-off-Broadway plays.

How did *Oleanna* come into your life?

DEBRA: I went to an open call for *Oleanna*, to understudy, and I got the part as the understudy. Then, after a few months of understudying, I had been rehearsing with David Mamet, who was putting in a new actress, and he offered me the part. So that's how I broke into it, as far as making money and making my living.

From there I just kept getting work as an actress, so I was able to make a living. I did a lot of theater. I did the Wendy Wasserstein play, *The Sisters Rosensweig*, and then I did the movie *The Heidi Chronicles* and I did the movie of *Oleanna* and I was doing television and TV movies – I moved out to Los Angeles.

But the business of acting was not good for me. I wasn't very happy and I didn't understand it. Nobody taught me, there's no book to prepare you for what it is. I had just been acting in classes, which I enjoyed. But auditioning for casting directors and dealing with agents – I was completely green. I had no idea how to deal with these people. I was pretty young, about twenty-three.

So I went to film school and I learned how to edit and I learned to do all the things you need to do to make a film. It really opened up a whole new world to me that I changed my life completely and I became a much happier person. Everything just fell into place in my life when I moved into film.

How did your low-budget feature, *The Limbo Room*, come about?

DEBRA: My sister and I had been working on a play. I really wanted to write a play about an understudy, because I had started understudying and it was this whole backstage world. The whole idea was just so bizarre to me: you're trapped backstage while this play is going on out there. And you're in this little room in the back and you have to listen to what's going on out on the stage and you may (or may not) go on. There are just so many metaphors going on within the idea of an understudy.

When I was doing *Oleanna*, I was the understudy. When I walked into that play, David Mamet's wife was the actress and she had been doing the play for a long time. And was suffering horribly from playing that role. Every night she got beat-up on stage and every night the audience would cheer. It's just a hated character. And I thought that I would be immune to that. I played that role in *Oleanna* for a year and I realized, in retrospect, that it really did depress the hell out of me, playing that role night after night.

So that was one element I was interested in: what's real and what's not real and how you take on the character – you are this character but you aren't this character. Then this whole microcosm that's happening backstage with the understudies and the actors.

So we wrote *The Limbo Room*; we finished it in a summer, and then I shot that film in nine days.

And then I edited it over the course of a year. As soon as I finished the rough cut, I went into labor and had my baby. Then it went to Slamdance and the Sundance Channel has played it. It won some awards, too, so it's not bad for nine days and $30,000 dollars.

What did you learn, as a filmmaker, from your work as an actress in the movie *Oleanna*?

DEBRA: I worked with David Mamet on the stage production; I had already done the play for a long time before I did the film. So it was like we were doing the play again when we did the film.

David's method of working with actors is very different than my way of working with actors. He just basically gave me three Super Objectives for each act, which is kind of genius. So he said, "In this Act, you're seeking help, in this one you're doing this, in this one you're doing that." And that was really the extent of it.

The thing that I learned the most from David was how he led. He's a great leader. And I think that's what I took away from it.

How did he demonstrate that?

DEBRA: It was the way he treated everyone. He treated everyone with the utmost respect. It was a very tight ship; everyone felt like they were part of what was happening, from craft service to the grips. Everyone felt like they were special.

I've been on sets where people are really unhappy and miserable and cursing the director because he's disrespectful. That's what I learned from David, the way he respected everyone. And I think that's probably one of the most important things to learn.

You're their director, and people are not going to work for you and do the things you ask them to do if they're feeling unappreciated. And he was really good at making everybody feel totally worthwhile and appreciated and important. That's a lesson that could be easily overlooked, but when I compare it to other situations where the director is just not really present and not making everyone feel important and appreciated, it definitely shows.

In the past, I've been in a situation on shooting a movie where the director is just really rude and really disrespectful to the actors. And everyone takes their break and that's what they're talking about, they're talking about how they're feeling they're being disrespected. And then it shows up in the scene. It's like a domino effect.

David's a very, very smart man and he knows exactly what he needs to do to make everybody feel good. I think that's his strongest thing as a director and that was the biggest lesson I learned on that film.

EDIE FALCO ON "JUDY BERLIN"

What the biggest difference between doing *The Sopranos* and doing an independent film?

EDIE: The budget on one episode of *The Sopranos* is higher than all the movies I've done, combined.

I know Eric Mendelsohn is a long-time friend. At what point in his process does he start to involve you?

EDIE: Usually he'll wait until a script is finished and then give it to me to read, which is what he did [with *Judy Berlin*]. After I read it and told him how much I loved it, he said "I would love for you to play the part of Judy." I was flabbergasted, because he had not said a word to me about it.

I've read everything he's ever done and given my feedback, so I assumed that that's what this was.

What's the advantage of doing a film like this with a long-time friend?

EDIE: A lot of the films I've done I've done with friends and family. The advantage is you go in there feeling no obligation to prove yourself. You're assuming that these people know who you are, at least socially if not more than that. There's a camaraderie and a trust that is inherent in just all of you being there together. I know they trust me and I trust them. It gets that all out of the way so we can get down to the work.

I know Eric kept you and Barbara Barrie (who plays Judy's mother) apart before you shot your first scene together. Did that help?

EDIE: It sure did. Although I thought it was just a matter of scheduling. I thought, 'All right, I won't meet her until the day we shoot.' That's the way these things are. I think in retrospect it did help.

She was a woman around whom I was unfamiliar. You hold your body differently; eye contact is different than with someone that you're comfortable around. I think physically the relationship that Judy and her mother had sort of mirrored that of strangers. In that regard, the subconscious stuff that was already taking place probably only fed what was happening in the script. And I imagine that was his intent.

Is your preparation any different when you know you're going into a lowbudget project?

EDIE: No, not at all. Really nothing about my preparation or involvement is any different on anything I do. The only thing that varies is, if I read something and I like it, I'll do it. If I read something and I don't like it, I won't. Once I've decided I'm doing something, I approach everything exactly the same, whether it's a play or a movie or a low-budget movie or a big budget movie. It's irrelevant.

How is working on a low-budget movie different?

EDIE: You get a lot of directors who are nervous, and they don't trust themselves or they don't trust the process. So, they might end up doing a lot more takes than they need, as if the actor is an infinite source of these things. Because at a certain point I know I'm not doing work that I'm proud of anymore, I'm just exhausted. And they are just too afraid to say, 'Okay, let's move on.' And so you'll do another four, five takes, and I start thinking, 'Oh, this is not what I meant to do, this is not the take I want.' So that's a little rough.

But once you start doing things where they put you in a nice trailer, and you've got people running around and taking care of you, when you all of a sudden have to change clothes in the back of a Chevy again, you think, 'You know, this does kind of stink, come to think of it. I would prefer to be in a trailer right now.'

So, I don't know if I've been a little bit spoiled by some of the bigger budget stuff. And you realize there's a reason you're taken care of, because you want to show up and do the best you can each time you're out there. It does help to be rested and warm and all that stuff.

There are so many advantages to working on a low-budget project. I feel a totally comfortable with the idea of trying something and having it not work. I feel a sense of freedom to just go for it, because money is not at the forefront of everything that goes on in these things. You don't have a producer standing over you saying, 'We gotta make the day!' Everybody's just flying by the seat of their pants and I feel a sense of freedom that I don't when money is being talked about.

Also, on a big-budget thing, there are a zillion people working on it. Oftentimes nobody knows who anybody else is and they don't necessarily care about their job, they're just trying to get enough days so they can become an AD.

On these low-budget things, everybody's there because they want to be. They know the director, they love the work of the director, they're a friend and he needed a helping hand. You know you're not going to make money and you know it's going to be hard work and you're there because you love it. And that is infused in every moment you spend on the set of a low-budget movie. It's been my experience that nothing but good stuff will come out of that.

Judy Berlin **has a really exceptional cast – Barbara Barrie, Bob Dishy, Madeline Kahn, Anne Meara, Julie Kavner. Was that intimidating at all?**

EDIE: No. At a certain point, if you've dealt with a bunch of these people, you realize that they really are just people. And when it comes down to who's talented and who's nice, that's all I'm really impressed by these days.

Barbara Barrie was, I'm sure, thrilled to get a script that was so good. Doesn't matter what the budget is. You see this big budget stuff that's being made, and you read the script and you're thinking, 'How did this happen to this industry?'

So you read a good script -- and my experience is, I don't care who's doing it, where it's being done, but I'd give my right arm to be involved in it. As far as I'm concerned, the most valued commodity in this industry is good writing. I was not at all surprised that he got the cast he did.

I was really sick for a good part of that shoot. We did mostly night shoots, because of the eclipse stuff, and I had a stomach virus. And I thought to myself, 'There's no way I can do this. There's just no way." And there was. I showed up and I felt sick and I was somehow able to get through the days. I was pleased to see that I can show up for stuff even when I think I can't.

Do you want to work with Eric again?

EDIE: I would do so in a heartbeat. At the core of our friendship is this frustration and sadness that he has such a hard time getting his movies made. He wants to shoot it in black and white and people are scratching their heads, going, 'How can I possibly put money into that? I'm never going to make it back.'

So, he's got a bunch of scripts, they're all brilliant and beautiful, and people are saying, 'Well, we're sorta interested, but re-write the ending.' And he's like, 'But that's not the story I want to tell.'

I would work with him again in a second if somebody would give him the money to make a movie.

MO COLLINS ON "MADTV" AND MORE ...

How did you get started in comedy?

MO: I don't have schooling beyond doing the Dudley Riggs Brave New Workshop classes for improv. I got started by just doing it. You just start.

When I was in school I learned some improv, and then, when I had no idea what I was going to do with my life, I remembered loving improv. I saw an ad in City Pages for classes, took the classes and before I knew it an agent called and then there was a check in the mail and I thought, "Well, I guess this is what I do."

How did you like the classes?

MO: It was great, because I finally realized where I belonged, which was with fellow comedy people. I learned how to improv and how to write.

A lot people who start in improv say that it provides a bedrock of learning for the rest of their careers. Was that the case for you?

MO: Absolutely, because the biggest thing that's learned there is the work ethic, which is what has carried me through. You really had to work hard there. You had to. You worked really hard and were paid very little. A great lesson, especially if you're headed to Hollywood.

But the work ethic was the biggest thing I learned at Dudley Riggs. So any other long day that came along later, I was used to it, because I started at Dudley at 20 and it's just in my blood that you do long days when you're working. But it's play, so you don't feel it.

And the Riggs experience also taught you how to write?

MO: It did some teaching of that, yes. I still hesitate to call myself any kind of a writer, but because I do improv, I am writing in mid air. But when you learn scene structure from improv -- beginning, middle and an end -- and character development, you kind of naturally get the writing skills that come along with it.

How did you use those skills once you left Riggs but before you moved to LA?

MO: Up there I was doing commercial work and industrial work and plays.

How would your improv skills come in handing while shooting an industrial video?

MO: Well, I was fearless. Improv is theater without a net, as we used to say, so anything else just seemed easy. And safe. Which isn't as fun. But when you have a sense of humor and go into these serious industrials that you're doing, to me it was just playing another comedy character, but playing it seriously.

The first thing I remember seeing you in was a part in a dinner theater mystery show ...

MO: Oh my gosh. Does that fall under acting or that waiting tables?

Then we cast you to play Lucille Ball in an industrial video. And even though you look nothing like her, you became Lucy.

MO: Because I understand what she's doing. It's funny, I just saw her show yesterday -- I hadn't watched Lucy in a while -- and as I was watching her I was noting to myself that I know exactly how she feels doing what she was doing. I understand how she got that performance. I totally got it. I could feel her rhythm and understand what she was doing. If that makes any sense at all.

I feel that I understand comedy so well; if there's something that I've studied in my years, it's comedy. I've been in all kinds of different groups of people who have a different comic tone, and I really do believe at this point that there's any camp of comedy that I could walk into and find my way.

I can feel it. I can feel what they're doing, even if it's not me or what I would naturally do.

As a for instances, I just did a pilot recently with David Cross and Bob Odenkirk. And they're a very different group. In fact, women aren't typically a part of that group. They're comedy nerds; they don't even know what to say to women. They don't. But I got in, because I knew how to make it safe for them to let me in and feel okay and not threatened. Not rock their boat but just come in and assimilate into what they're doing, because I understand their geek comedy. I can do it too. And I think it's just because, ultimately, I am a mocking bird. That's what I'm doing. I'm mimicking what they're doing and putting it into my body, my person, my mouth.

What made you decide to move to LA?

MO: I had a two year-old son. And I knew that Minneapolis was only going to allow me to do so well. I was doing okay, making a living, paying my mortgage, but that was going to continue on an even plane, instead of an upward climb. And I didn't want that. I knew that I could do more; I just knew it. And it wasn't going to happen in Minneapolis.

So what was your plan?

MO: To make it.

So like on the top of a piece of paper: "Day One: Make it."

MO: Yes, I'm going to go and I'm going to do this and it's going to work. And with in nine months I had *Mad TV*.

I knew I had something. So you just do it until you're seen. By the right person. And that's what happened.

I had done a play called *Cabin Pressure*, with a bunch of women from Minneapolis. We collaborated on this project, a really quirky comedy that we put together and put up on a stage out here. A casting director saw my character and she just jumped on board the Mo ship. She told the *Mad TV* casting people about me and I got the audition.

I knew, when the audition came, that I was going to get it.

How come?

MO: Because that's exactly what my resume is. It's exactly what I do. I was ready for it. Everything I had done had prepared me for that audition.

I knew, because I had taken a leap of faith, that I would be rewarded. You don't take such big leaps without rewards; I don't think the universe really works like that. I just knew it was going to work out.

It's funny, there were six auditions, and during the fifth one they sent me home early. And I thought it was a horrible mistake. I went home and I was crying and I thought, "They've made a terrible mistake. I'm going to get this. Somebody made a mistake."

Why did they send you home?

MO: Because they already knew they were going to cast me and didn't want to waste any more of my time that day. But I just wanted to stay and play. I wanted to show them more: "I've got more!"

How did the first show feel?

MO: It was thrilling and terrifying, because television wasn't something I knew, at all. I didn't know how television worked; that wasn't something I had experience at from Minneapolis. Commercial work is not television.

Things like, when the first AD starts the countdown ("Five, four, three ...") and then he doesn't say "One." I didn't know that he was just being quiet. And I had the first line, the first entrance in my first scene, and I didn't know. Nobody told me how that works.

I decided to fake it 'til I make it. And it worked out fine. But that was a learning process.

How were you used and how did you want to be used and how did you influence how you wanted to be used on the show?

MO: There's a lot of nuancing my position on *Mad TV* because there are politics involved and I'm a nice Minnesota girl and an easy door-mat. I had to stand on my talent because I wasn't a squeaky wheel as far as saying "Use me more!" That kind of stuff. "How come she's got this and I don't?" I just wasn't that person. And I watched as that didn't work. I watched as the squeaky wheel got the oil and that was really hard for me.

This was where I started to see that Hollywood didn't always function through talent. That talent wasn't what always propelled one forward and upward. And that's a really, really tough lesson. And potentially fatal to a career. But I decided not to let it kill me.

I learned how to stand my ground enough, and stay nice at the same time. And I let my work ethic, my non-complaining, my always showing up with my work ready and my characters full-bored. I kept growing my arsenal of things I could do and add to the show. And I kept growing. And the audience started to pick up on that and writing into the show and saying, "She's good. More her."

One of the things that sets you apart -- and above -- others in your field is your absolute commitment to each character you played. How did you build and grow that ability?

MO: I really love playing characters and taking them as far as I can. Really it's just a self-discovery that's happening within the performance. I'd get a script and there would be an image that would come to mind or a voice or something -- a character just starts. And by the time I'd chosen a wig or wardrobe or whatever, you're looking in the mirror and you see this character emerge. And that's fun. It's dress up. It's play time. And I'm just really good at playing.

Did you ever get to a point where you thought, enough already, I've got no more characters in me?

MO: I did always try to do something, even if it was just for three lines in a scene, I would think, "I'm going to make a person here, that fits in this scene and serves this scene."

On one of my last shows there was this scene and I thought, "I'm just going to go at this completely differently. I'm not going to think about an internal person. I am just going to make one of the ugliest faces I can make, I'm going to throw on the ugliest wig that they have, and just do that." Because a lot of people come at characters from that external place; they'll throw on some character glasses or whatever. But for me, there's a person in there that I can kind of feel when I read a script.

But in this case I went at it completely externally. It was really fun, I was like a kid, just making faces with this wig on. And it turned out to be a really fun character that people loved. Her name was Carol Fitty and I did her for a game show sketch. And then when they invited me back, after I'd left the show, they had me do her again.

So even in my trying not to do a character, a person emerged, which is pretty funny. And it was really fun for me to go at it so differently.

Were you in a position to bring in ideas for characters and sketches?

MO: You had to. You had to every week. It was part of the job. You'd dip into the writers room, pitch ideas, talk about a character or a thought. You had to do that.

Did you like doing that?

MO: Yeah I did. It scared me a little bit, too, because I felt like, they're the writers and who am I?

But you'd been writing on your feet for years. Why would you find that intimidating?

MO: Because I'm also insecure and will over-think something when I'm not on a stage. So I'd think, "This will be funny. I'll take it in tomorrow." And then the insecurity goes, "That's not funny, they're not going to like it, they're not going to get it." Whereas, if I'm on a stage and I'm doing it in an improv sketch, I know I can make it work. It's different telling, I'm much better at showing. It can be intimidating.

At what point did you decide to leave the show?

MO: Six seasons felt just about right. And I think you should do something else before Hollywood thinks you can't do anything else. You can get really trapped in the sketch world and once you do sketch, they say, "Oh, you're a sketch actor. You're not an actor." Especially if you're a woman.

SUSAN COYNE ON "SLINGS & ARROWS"

How did *Slings & Arrows* come about?

SUSAN COYNE: Well, I hadn't really set out to be a writer. But, I hit my late thirties, and I had two children and I couldn't travel across the country in the same way. And, famously, the parts thin out a bit as you get older.

So I sort of hit my mid-life crisis and thought, "I'm just going to sit down and start writing," without really knowing where it was going to lead me. And then I got hooked up with somebody who said, "You know, I have a friend who works at Stratford and loves hearing your stories. Would you like to come up with a proposal for a TV series about Stratford?"

So I said, "Sure. I can do that." And then I came up with the premise for the series, basically, although at that time it was a half-hour comedy. We shopped it around and we got wonderful producers, Rhombus Media, involved and they put me together with Mark McKinney of *Kids in the Hall*, which was really kind of brilliant.

That was an interesting choice.

SUSAN COYNE: He was not the first person you'd think of pairing us with, but it was really great because Mark is so smart and really thinks outside the box constantly. He's worked a little bit in theater and so he knew something of this world as well. He said right away, "This isn't a half-hour, this is an hour, because there's too much good material here."

I think that was one of the most important things that happened, because we thought, "We're doing Shakespeare, we don't want this to be just punch lines and then cut to a commercial. We want to be brave about this and tackle what it's like to do these big plays."

I'd never seen something like this done very well. I'd often seen actors made fun of, and it's easy. It's easy to satirize actors. I think we do it to a degree in the show. It's also easy to sentimentalize. But between those two extremes I've never seen anybody try to really show what it's like, and that in some ways it certainly matters to the people who do it and it might even mean something to those of us who watch. It might have some value, it might have some weight to it, it might not be a silly thing to do with your life. And that these people might have some passion that has some dignity to it.

Even as I say that I'm always cautious not to give it more weight than it's worth, but I think that when theater works well, everybody recognizes that there's something very powerful about it, transforming and ineffable and not silly at all. It's rare, but when you see it, there's nothing like it. You feel a little bit wrung out afterwards and your heart's beating faster and you feel chemically altered in some way.

It's that we wanted to get at: What is that thing that happens and how do people achieve that? We wanted to show people the kinds of conversations that go on in rehearsals as well as how terrifying it is and the ridiculous things we do to get ourselves where we have to be. All of that.

I always think that when there's a great deal of passion, then there's got to be some kind of dramatic or comic story. Or both.

How did Bob Martin get involved?

SUSAN COYNE: Bob was invited to join Mark and I after we had been wrestling with the series for a couple of years (in the midst of doing other projects- in my case, co-founding a theatre company and writing my first book). Neither Mark nor I had written a TV series before, but Bob had. His experience was the key to making us into a fully functioning writing team.

When you started the project, did you think it would only be for one season?

SUSAN COYNE: Exactly. Mark and I worked for a couple of years, because we were both doing other things. And it took a long time to figure out how this was going to go. We had six episodes in mind, we knew the play was *Hamlet*, we came up with the idea of the ghost and that our character was going to be a sort of Hamlet figure who was haunted almost in the same way that I was haunted by my theater school teachers. The ones who said those wonderful things and those terrible things, and you're always trying to prove something to them even if they're dead.

It turns out that three is a good number for a writing team, because we could always gang up on the other person and persuade them. The three-legged writing team is quite stable, actually. If you can't quite see something, one of the other two can explain it to you. And also Bob had real experience writing television in a way that Mark and I didn't. And he also has an amazing comic sensibility and a really delightful wit.

So when that came together the work started to go faster and we decided that six episodes would be really satisfying to tackle *Hamlet*. And that really was the plan until we finished it and watched it. The network said, would you like to go another year? And we looked at each other and I said, "Well, I think we should do a trilogy. If we're going to another one we should do three and we should do youth, middle-age and old age." That made sense to us and felt like it would be a satisfying arc.

We had the idea that, each season, we wanted to watch our characters through the filter of the play -- not in the way that you could draw straight lines between the stories and the play, but in a sort of general way being influenced by Shakespearean themes.

One of my favorite scenes in the series -- and one that really lays Shakespeare out and explains what's he's doing -- is the scene in the first season when the director, Geoffrey, explains to the actress playing Ophelia exactly what her "nonsense rhymes" actually mean. Did you find that there were scenes you created based on things you'd actually experienced?

SUSAN COYNE: There were. But some of them are so disguised that they take on a difference resonance. For example, Geoffrey reminds me of a director I worked with early on who directed me in *The Glass Menagerie*. He was a refugee from the Second World War, a Holocaust survivor. His family perished, and he escaped to Winnipeg. He talked to me about how theater had saved his life, and it meant so much to me, the way he talked about it. It was a life force for him.

I guess there's an element where I've worked with really great directors for whom theater has saved their life. And that passion for its humanity -- for the idea of theater being a place where we can be very human with each other -- is something that I've retained, and I always aspire to in the theater. The idea that it's about people communicating; there's no tricks, there's no cinema, it's just us. We're all in the same room breathing together, and if it all works out, we'll all end up having the same heart-rate at the end of the show.

Were you saddled with handling the female point of view on the show and the female characters or was that shared?

SUSAN COYNE: Oh it was definitely shared. Martha Burns, who plays Ellen, is one of my closest friends. We've known each other a long time, we grew up in Winnipeg together, so I loved coming up with storylines for her, like Ellen getting audited. But we all wrote the Ellen character and we all wrote the Anna character.

I loved aspects of Anna, but the boys, actually, I think loved Anna even more. They loved putting her in these terrible situations. The scene where she had to have sex, Mark wanted it to be really explicit and hardcore, and I finally said, "Look, guys, it's me playing the part. So let's just re-think this, shall we?"

And that's when Bob said, "Well, we could do it in the dark." I said "That sounds very good."

Do you have any special or favorite moments from the series?

SUSAN COYNE: I loved everything to do with Bill Hutt in the third season. I was in a production of *Lear* with him, at Stratford in the young company, and he is a hero of mine. He's gone now, and his Lear was never filmed. So to get the little bit that we get of him, doing the great speeches, that I feel proudest of, actually.

That is the most important thing to me about the series: that we got him. We always wanted him; we wanted him in the second season and he wasn't available. But we got him in the third season. And then within 18 months he had died. So it was amazing. He was such a wonderful guy and he threw himself into it. I loved that.

Other than that, there was a tiny moment, backstage in the second season, between Geoffrey and Ellen, where they're watching *Romeo and Juliet*. And Ellen says, "I hate this play." I must say, watching *Romeo and Juliet* as a middle-aged person, you watch it and you think, "I hate this play." I mean, I love it of course, but you're in such a different headspace from the first time you played it, you can't help thinking, "What, are you nuts?"

What did you take away from the *Slings & Arrows* experience?

SUSAN COYNE: I learned a lot from working with two other people whose sensibilities were similar to mine, but who also pushed me ways into places I otherwise never would have gone. Although we fought a lot at the beginning, we got into a place where it was much easier to say, "Here's a sketch of the scene, but you should write it because you have that voice down better." It became very respectful -- and although there were still fights, they were good fights; not pulling in different directions, but creative fights -- where you just knew that the other person, it was just their thing and they could write it better. And you knew that when it came time to take over another scene, they would say, "You should have a go at that."

I think that's hard to replicate, when you have developed a working relationship like that with people.

As for the acting, that was more intimidating. Film is socially so different from theater. You don't have an audience; the only person who's actually watching your performance is the director, because everyone else is watching other things, like how your scarf is tied. So I found that a bit intimidating.

But there was a very collegial feeling, and we had so many theater actors coming onto the set, and so it felt much more about the work than it usually does. That was very freeing for me, because I've always felt that I'm very uptight on the set and never felt very free. And so to be with this wonderful team, on a series that you created yourself, playing this lovely character was wonderful. I adored playing Anna.

PART IV
THE VP OF PRODUCTION

DONNA SMITH

Let's start with a clarification to make sure I have this right: In the history of Hollywood, you are the only woman to run physical production at a studio, in this case at Universal Pictures. Is that right?

DONNA: Can you imagine? Over a hundred years in Hollywood there had never been a woman in charge of physical production at a studio. A distressing fact.

You're a Minnesotan like myself. What brought you to Hollywood and to the movies?

DONNA: You know what the answer is? The weather. And that's the absolute truth.

I had been very fortunate in my Minneapolis working days, because I worked for five years at the Walker Art Center and I worked for five years at The Guthrie Theater. So how much more blessed can anybody be if you're interested in working in the performing arts or in culture in general? It was like freeloading two educations, one in modern art and then one in classical theater. And I worked directly with Tyrone Guthrie; I was his assistant for three years.

So the weather drove you out of Minnesota?

DONNA: Yes. I met my husband, Gordon, at The Guthrie. I remember this: It was May and Gordon came home from the theater and he walked in and he said, "If one more fucking snowflake falls on me in the month of May, I'm going to lose my mind!" It was May and it was snowing. And he just couldn't believe it; he was so insulted by that. I remembering looking at him and saying, "You're not emotionally fit to live here anymore."

And we actually moved within that year. We both had very nice employment and beautiful jobs at the Guthrie Theater -- he'd been there since the inception. He was the very first employee; he was a stage manager who came from New York.

So we did move. Gordon said to me, "Do you want to move to New York or Los Angeles?" And my answer was, "Not New York." I never had a heartbeat for New York. Every time I go to New York, even now, I want to stay five days and get out of there. I don't like the energy, I don't like the noise, I don't like the pollution.

So we went on what we called our Odyssey and when we left Minneapolis we took a year to get to California, until our money ran out. We traveled with the sun and went all around the U.S., Canada and Mexico to get here.

I remember we were in Seattle and I said, "We have $11.00 left. We have to get to Los Angeles." And it was true, we only had $11.00.

And along the way we had picked up a cat in Carlsbad Caverns, New Mexico, I found a little baby cat. So here was the cat traveling in the van with us with a litter box. It was kind of a hoot. I didn't mind but Gordon objected. Carl was my cat, he lived with us for 12 years.

So we arrived here in Los Angeles with a van we'd been traveling in and Carl the cat and Gordon and Donna. Total unemployment. We didn't know anybody in Los Angeles. And we had eleven bucks.

So you'd landed in Los Angeles ... how did you find work?

DONNA: I went to an employment agency and said, "I'm kind of smart and know how to do things, and I've got a very organized mind. I have a great sense of detail. And I come from the theater!" I was so proud of that, and they said, "Go fish. We couldn't care less. Theater doesn't mean anything in this town."

It was so awful. But this lady said, "I don't care how good you are. We have one thing here, for an assistant filing clerk." And I remember saying, "Assistant filing clerk? That's a little beneath what I had in mind. I worked with Sir Tyrone Guthrie and all."

Not even a filing clerk, but an assistant filing clerk.

DONNA: And only for two weeks. Some lady was behind in her filing and she needed someone for two weeks. So I said, "Oh, good grief. All right, I'll take it." I didn't know anybody, I didn't know what else to do.

So she handed me a card and said "Go to this address tomorrow." And that's all that I had. It could have been a company that sold tires, I had no idea, the name meant nothing to me. So I went to the address, it was in Culver City, and I checked in. I worked for this really mean lady. She said, "Sit down over there and get this stuff filed!" She just had the personality of a snake; she was so abrupt, yelling and not nice.

So I sat down and she gave me this big stack of purchase orders. It meant nothing to me, they were just purchase orders and all I was doing was filing them by number. I didn't read them or anything.

But it was serendipity, really.

On about the fourth day, I looked up because I heard this voice, and I thought, "Oh my god, there's Rocky. What's Rocky doing here?" It's a very distinctive voice. And I looked up and there was Sylvester Stallone on the other side of the office. And I thought, "What's he doing here? This is so exciting," because the movie Rocky had recently come out and he was on the cover of Time magazine.

It was pretty exciting to see him. I didn't say anything to the mean lady, I just told Gordon on the phone that night, "Guess what, I saw

Rocky today!" I didn't know his real name, by the way, he was just Rocky.

And then two days later, there was Travis Bickle. And I thought, "There's Travis Bickle, what's going on here?"

So it's Robert DeNiro.

DONNA: It's Robert DeNiro. So I told Gordon that night on the phone, "I saw Travis Bickle today, he was in this office." And Gordon said, "What is this place," and I said, "I don't know."

But the next day I had the guts finally to ask the mean lady, "What does this company do?" And she turned around with her hands on her hips and said, "We make movies."

And I sat down and thought, "They make movies? How do you make a movie?" I couldn't ask her anything because she was so mean and nasty, so I just pondered that all day. And at least I realized, then, why Travis and Rocky were there.

Well the name of the company on the card just simply said Chartoff-Winkler. It meant nothing to me. Like I said, they could have sold tires instead.

This was the company that made *Rocky*. That's why Sly was there, working on *Rocky II*. And that's why Bobby was there, because he had just finished *Taxi Driver* with them. It was amazing.

Then on about day eight of my ten days, the man who the mean lady reported to (she turned out to be the Production Coordinator, working for the Production Manager), he came by me and said, "You. Come in. Take notes. I'm going to have a meeting." So I was just sort of wide-eyed, but I went into the meeting -- I had never been at a meeting in this place, I was just doing purchase orders -- and I wrote down every word he said.

His name was Jim Brubaker, he was the Production Manager. He said, "We've already shot Rocky II, but Sly hates the ending and we're going to re-do it. So we need to get 3,000 extras, we need to get the sports arena back, we need to have all the principles ..." and he just rattled all this stuff off.

And I'm writing notes like crazy. And he pointed at me and said, "This is Donna Smith, she'll be the Production Coordinator. And this is Benjy Rosenberg, he's the first A.D. Coordinate everything with them. This fucking meeting's over."

And I remember writing down that word, "fucking," and I just couldn't believe it because we don't talk that way in Minnesota. And I was just so alarmed and I wrote that word down and I actually missed the part where he said "This is Donna Smith, she'll be the Production Coordinator."

I went up to Brubaker after and I tugged on his sleeve like a four-year old and I said, "Mr. Brubaker, you said my name, I think you made a mistake." He said, "No, I haven't made a mistake. I've been watching you. You can do it, but if you don't want to do it, I'll get someone else."

And I said, "No, no, no, I can do it. I just didn't understand."

Then Mean Lady came up to me and said, "You just took my job!" And I looked at her and said, "Oh my god, if that's what happened, I'm not aware of it." And she honestly cut me a break. She said, "I'm not going to hold it against you, because you're so green. I know you didn't go after it." And it was true, I really didn't go after it.

The next day I came back to that company and I was sitting there at her desk, looking at the Production Coordinator placard she had on the desk, thinking, "Yep, it says Production Coordinator. Yep, that's what it says." I didn't know diddly. I didn't know one thing about what to do.

Then people started coming up to me, asking questions. And I wrote everything down. I'd just sit there and say, "I'll get back to you on that." And that was okay, nobody seemed to mind if I said that.

What did you do then?

DONNA: Well, then you start trying to find out what the answers are.

There was a pivotal moment. A guy came up to me, I didn't know who it was, and he said, "Hey, toots, what emulsion are we on?" So I said, "I'll get back to you on that." And he said, "Okay" and just walked away.

So I called the drugstore, because I remembered that the word "emulsion" was on the can of film that you brought into the drugstore at that time. It had that word on it. So I called the drugstore and I said, "Hello, this is Donna Smith, I'm the Production Coordinator on the *Rocky II* re-shoots. Do you know what 'emulsion' means?" And the guy said, "Lady, who do you think I am? Kodak?" And he hung up on me.

And I thought, "Oh. Interesting." So I got the Yellow Pages out and I looked it up and there was a Kodak in Los Angeles, and I thought, "I'll call them up and see if they know something."

So I called Kodak and said, "Hello, this is Donna Smith, I'm the Production Coordinator on the Rocky II re-shoots. Do you know what emulsion we're on?" The guy said, "Hold on a moment," and then he came back and he said, "5247."

I thought, "Well, I can do this job. It's just reasoning. It's sense of detail. I'll just teach myself, because this Brubaker guy isn't going to tell me anything and the Mean Lady is gone."

I would never have called Kodak if the drugstore guy hadn't hung up on me.

And then when I saw the man who asked me about the emulsion again, I said, "Sir, it's 5247." And he said, "Okay," and he walked away. And as he walked away, I said, "Sir, sir!" And he turned around, and I said, "Don't ever call me 'toots' again." And he looked at me and said, "Fuckin' A."

And I was just thrilled but also stymied, thinking, "Oh my god, how am I going to handle these people. These people are horrible."

But unbeknownst to me, he went to the crew (I found out later) and told them, "Don't mess with the new Production Coordinator. She's really tough and she knows what she's doing." What a snow job that was.

At the end of the *Rocky II* re-shoots, Brubaker came up to me and said, "You're really good. I want you to work with me on my next film." And I said, "A whole movie?" And he said,

"Well of course it's a whole movie! For god's sake!" He thought it was so stupid on my part, to talk about a whole movie.

So he said, "Yes, it's a whole movie." And he gave me this script and said, "Read this." And guess what it was? *Raging Bull*. That's why Bobby was there, getting ready for *Raging Bull* with Chartoff-Winkler. So Brubaker was the Production Manager and I was the Production Coordinator on *Raging Bull*.

That's how it all started, kiddo. In great detail, that's how it all started.

So you were self taught?

DONNA: Oh yeah. No college degree on that.

Was your theater background any help?

DONNA: Very little, kiddo. I'm sure it did more than I remember now, but in many ways not really. Because now I'm working with things called Call Sheets and Production Reports and Film Reports and Footage Shot and all these forms that a Coordinator gets handed to do. And all the SAG rules, and I'm walking around saying to myself, "What doe SAG mean, everybody's talking about SAG. I have to post a SAG bond, what the heck does that mean?"

I was in so over my head at that time, but I retained every single thing I learned. And I brought everything home. I think to this day Brubaker has no idea, but I brought everything home at night and Gordon, God love him, was a real good sport. We would sit at the dining room table and I remember going over all these forms -- because it's all forms -- and trying to figure it out.

And then I started reading all those purchase orders I had been filing. I'm reading about Baby Ks and a 5K, and I'm thinking, "What's a 5K?" I didn't know any of it and none of it came from theater, none of the lingo or the language came from theater.

So, in reality, the employment people could have sent you to a tire company and you would now be an expert in the tire business.

DONNA: This is true. I would know tire measurements.

It really worked out. *Raging Bull*, of all movies to land on for the first one, I just learned and learned and learned. And I was good at it. I could really keep up with it, I understood it, the flow of it.

It was such a huge, huge film shoot to be on, and then it won the Academy Award and turned out to be the best film of the decade, and you think, "Wow. I did that."

What happened next?

DONNA: Then Brubaker and I did *True Confessions* right after that. That was Robert DeNiro again and Robert Duvall. And guess what? Ulu Grosbard directed it. So I was going, "I know Ulu Grosbard! He's a theater dude. And he's married to Rose." I knew all of that.

And everyone in Hollywood was saying, "Who's this guy? What's his name? Where did he come from?" But I was one person who knew. "Ulu, how are you? And how's Rose?" And blah, blah, blah. Everyone else thought I'd walked off the moon because nobody knew him.

So I did *True Confessions* with Brubaker and I just never stopped working. I somehow just landed on one picture after the other.

The phone kept ringing.

DONNA: The phone honestly kept ringing. I never went to unemployment. I learned on the first movie that during the last week of employment everybody goes to the unemployment office and signs up. And that was my measure of success.

Then I had a call from a Canadian, a guy who called and said, "I hear you're good." I remember I had a smart mouth, and I said, "Is this a sexual call?" Isn't that awful?

But his name was Lou Lehman and he was the president of the DGC, the Directors Guild of Canada. And Lou knew my husband, Gordon. Lou called and said that he was directing a movie and they were filming -- you're going to love this -- in Beaver Dam, Wisconsin. And I said, "I know where that is."

He said, "I want you to come and be the Production Manager. We've already started filming. We've got a Production Manager, but I've got to fire him, he's no damn good. And I want you to be my Production Manager."

And I remember thinking, "Wow. Production Manager. I've only done three movies, how can I be a Production Manager already?" But I thought, if I do this for a Canadian shoot, in Beaver Dam, Wisconsin, maybe nobody in Hollywood will know if I fall on my face.

So I took the job. And I remember flying to Beaver Dam, Wisconsin on a Sunday. I was reading the script and I told him, "I just have to be off limits for a couple of days, so I can read the paperwork and find out what's going on." That's when I found it was Canadian Union, and I didn't know any of the Canadian Union rules. And if you're a Production Manager and you don't know the rules, the crew can just gobble you up and spit you out.

So I knew I had to learn the rules. I was trying so hard to absorb all those rules, and then there was a knock at the door. I answered the door and there was a guy who just took up the entire doorframe. He stood there and he said, "So, are you Miss Hollywood?" And I looked at him and I said, "No, I don't think .... yeah, yeah I am. What do you want?"

And he said, "All I want to know, lady, is -- it's Sunday, it's my day off. The truck's not working. Do I go fix the fuckin' truck or do I go bowling with the boys?"

I knew this was a huge test. So I said to this guy, "You must be a grip. You go bowling with the boys. I'll fix the fuckin' truck." And I slammed the door in his face.

That was the best thing to do. The word got around to that crew was I pretty severe. But I still had to get the truck fixed!

It was really tough, but it made me have to be, well, I guess tough is the word. But still I never wanted to lose my femininity. That was so important to me to not start saying that word and talking like the boys and scratching my balls. I just absolutely didn't want to be that way.

I'm five-four, just a normal-sized girl, and most Production Managers are tall and have booming voices. I didn't have that going for me. So I tried to figure out what am I going to do to just have a little distinction? So I decided on wearing suspenders. And I wore suspenders every day on every shoot after that. I bought a bunch of them.

A ball cap -- everybody's got a ball cap on. That didn't stand out. But if you wear suspenders, then you stand out. It was a very subtle thing for me, but that became my signature piece.

A good theatrical choice.

DONNA: Yes, you're right. A very theatrical choice.

So you never made a resume and never went to unemployment.

DONNA: I never made a resume. I remember after Beaver Dam I came back to town and I had three scripts to read, which was a blessing. I turned out to be a really good Production Manager, but all of a sudden I'm back in Los Angeles after that and nobody knows me. I'm not union. And I had the best attitude in town, because I said, "I guess I'm a Production Coordinator again." And I was.

I just went right back into being Production Coordinator and got instant work with three scripts from three different production managers who knew about my earlier work.

So, is it safe to say that if you're good at what you do in Hollywood, eventually the work will come to you?

DONNA: I'm an absolute product of that. I never, ever wrote a resume. I never had to shop shows. And I never went to unemployment. I always had another movie lined up after the one I was working on.

So it was more than just luck?

DONNA: I never considered myself lucky. I consider myself fortunate but not lucky, because I worked really hard. Plus I had to prove myself. I had to learn so much and I had to stay hired. That was a big deal for me, to stay hired.

So then I did three movies in a row with Scott Rudin -- later he turned out to be SCOTT RUDIN, but he wasn't so much SCOTT RUDIN then.

After that I did become Production Manager on two non-union pictures in town. Everything always went well. I never had any problems; never over budget, nothing bad.

And then I got a call from this guy in England who said he had a completion bond company and he wanted me to come head it up here in Los Angeles. And I thought, "Well, here's another piece of the business I don't know anything about."

All of a sudden a steady salary, not working picture to picture. And I don't think I considered myself a filmmaker yet. I really did become one, but I don't think I considered myself to be one then.

For the uninitiated, exactly what is a bond company?

DONNA: As the bond company, you have to make sure that each movie is finished. You promise completion. That's the biggest thing, that you're going to complete the movie and deliver it to whoever is getting it, and that it will be on-time and on-budget. And if it isn't, if there's any claim from the production company ("Sorry about that, we went $800,000 over budget, so you have to pay it"), that's why I'm there. To make sure that never happens. And, believe me, it never happened.

But if a claim is placed, that's what's expected of you as a bond company. You have to complete it because you've got your name on it that you will promise to complete it, and then you'd put in your own money.

My first rule, which I developed on the second day at the bond company, was that we were never going to put our money into somebody else's movie. How stupid would that be? I just looked at it as a basic, maybe Minnesotan way of looking at it, as opposed to the Hollywood way of looking at it. I realized that it was our obligation, but I also knew it was something we were never going to do. I'm not going to put this company's money into somebody else's movie; to me that's just stupid.

So how do you achieve that goal?

DONNA: You become the sheriff who really watches the movie. I watched dailies. I insisted that I watch everybody's dailies.

So as a bond company, what are you watching for when you look at dailies?

DONNA: I'm watching for things that the filmmakers don't realize. I'm looking for the clapper and if I see Take 27, then I'm all over it. None of the filmmakers would ever know that, as the bond company, that's why I'm looking at dailies. They think I'm looking for artistic integrity.

Well, I want to make sure that the right words are being said and that we're completing the script pages that have to be shot, that I'm watching for very definitely. But I had also learned so much about filmmaking that I'm particularly watching for the clapper.

I would be all over them: "Right now you're getting ready to stray off the reservation, and I'm here to tell you that you're not straying off the reservation. This is what your obligation is and no more money is going to be sent to you; nobody's enhancing your movie. You do it right or I'll make sure you never work in Hollywood again." That kind of attitude -- I'd never literally say that to them. But you just have to scare them.

Nobody could start a project until me (the bond company) had read the script, critiqued it (we'd say things like, "Get this scene out of there, it's not needed and it's going to cost too much."). We look at the budget and see if they were under budget, or over budget, or we could see the pads in their budget.

And then we'd go over the schedule. I would read and sign off on all of that. Nobody got a green light until I was completely comfortable that all that had happened. And then part of my deal was that the first check you write, as soon as you get your cash flowing, is a complete check to the bond company for the fee. None of this half and half, no thirds, nothing like that. One check, your first check, to the bond company.

Hearing that, it just strikes me that someone in that position

would have to have just a tremendous amount of knowledge about the film business and how movies are made to take on that role.

DONNA: You know what? I think I agree with you.

So, if I'm doing the math right here, you'd been in the film business -- from 1978 to 1982 when you started at the bond company -- for a total of only about four years at that point. That's a pretty meteoric leap to make in just four years.

DONNA: I've never thought of that. But I really did learn filmmaking in that time. And I had not one day of training for the job. You just get thrown in the deep end and you learn it while you're there.

When Tyrone Guthrie offered me the job at the Guthrie Theater, I told him, "But I don't know how to do anything." And he looked at me and said, "Well dear, don't worry about that. I do."

You two must have been quite a pair, you at 5' 4" and he was, what, 6' 6"?

DONNA: That's right, 6' 6", and he only wore his bedroom slippers.

So what made you decide to leave the bond company?

DONNA: The owner decided to sell the company. So that's what put me back on the marketplace.

The guys at Hemdale knew me from being their bond lady. So when they decided to green light The Terminator -- Jim Cameron and Gale Anne Hurd had had a hell of a time finding anyone to let them do that movie -- Hemdale introduced them to me.

I remember Gordon and I went to Florida that Christmas and I said, "I have three scripts to read, three different offers, but one of them is sci-fi." And he said, "Oh, honey, don't even read it," because I don't get sci-fi. My mind can just never get around sci-fi.

And later I told him, "Well, I've read all these scripts and I know which one I want to do." And he said, "Which one?" And I said, "The sci-fi." He said, "Oh, Donna, you can't do that. You don't understand it." And I said, "I know, but it's so well written."

So I decided to do *The Terminator*. I went back to work and I was Production Manager on The Terminator because it was non-union. I worked my butt off on that movie. And the biggest thing was that Jim Cameron wanted to be JIM CAMERON at that time.

The job in itself was huge, because of all the effects, but Jim trying to become JIM was a huge alligator to wrestle on the side.

I remember our first fight. We were shooting and finished a shot and he said, "That's perfect. Let's do it again." And I went up to him and said, "Excuse me. Come to the side, please, so I can talk to you."

And then I said, "Jim you just said 'That was perfect. Let's do it again.' It doesn't work that way. If it's perfect, we've got it. You say, 'Ladies and gentlemen, we're on the wrong set. Set- up for the next one because this one is finished. We got the shot, it was perfect, we're moving on.'"

And he was ready to just sink his fangs into me. But lesson learned -- you don't say, "That was perfect, let's do it again." It doesn't work that way.

Did he stop doing that?

DONNA: Well, my stories and Jim's stories would probably be hugely different. I knew that I hadn't crossed a line with that, but it was a real dicey thing, because I have to get along with this guy for a long time, because I had also signed on as Post-Production Supervisor on that film, so I was going to have Jim in my life for a year.

I had a t-shirt made up for him the next day. On the front it said, "That was perfect." And on the back it said, "Let's do it again." I gave him the t-shirt as a sort of love offering.

So let's jump ahead: How did you go from Production Manager on The Terminator to running Universal?

DONNA: As *The Terminator* became a big, international hit, I went off to Europe to do my first European movie. I was in Yugoslavia and didn't really know what was going on back in the States. But I had to leave Yugoslavia all the time to go to Zurich, to get money every week. And while I was there I'd see the ads and the billboards for *The Terminator*, and I'd think, "Yeah, I worked on that movie." It was just kind of fun.

And then, whoa, as you went around Europe it was all over the place. That was great fun, to have done that and to be in Europe and see the European take on it all. I missed everything in the States because I was gone.

But then I worked in Europe a lot, probably five movies in a row. And now I had other titles, like Executive in Charge of Production, and Line Producer, and Grand Fromage, and all these other titles, because I was always non-union. So even though I was working on union shoots, I couldn't get the Unit Production Manager credit, because that was dictated by the DGA. So I would be the UPM, but I'd get all these other titles because of that complication.

I had always thought that was going to be a big handicap for me, but I somehow made the list of hotshot Production Managers. Then I'd tell them that I wasn't union and that would kind of cause a problem. But if they wanted me, we always made it work out.

When I came back to the States I thought, "Oh, I'm never going to work again, because nobody's going to remember me."

And then I did what even I'll say was the most clever thing: I'd never done a resume and I was just frightened about never getting hired again.

So I had a booklet made up at the printers, a spiral notebook about three by five. On the front page I had my name and phone number, and on the cover of the booklet -- it was a black cover -- I had written in gold, "Non-Union Rules & Regulations."

I sent it to every production company in town, I sent it to everybody. I had such a great response. It would arrive on their desks, and they'd say, "Oh, man I've been waiting to get a book like this! This is fantastic!" And then they'd open it up and it was all blank pages.

If I sent it out to three hundred companies, I got phone calls from a hundred and fifty of them. "You've got to come in and meet me." "I've been hearing about you." "You're the best broad in town."

Everybody in town was buzzing about that and I had all these interviews. And I was just never without work.

Then I did the movie *K9*.

K9 was a full Universal movie, and here I am again, the non-union Production Manager. Actually, at that point, I was more of a Line Producer, a term we use a lot now but we weren't really using it then.

So Universal wanted me to do that movie. Larry and Chuck Gordon were the producers and I was good friends with them. I really adored them; tough to work for, but we had a very fine working relationship.

Larry really wanted me to do that movie, so he called me about it and I said "Terrific," and I was available. And then -- this is fun -- I hired Jim Brubaker as the Production Manager. Isn't that something?

So Brubaker was the Production Manager and I was the Grand Fromage and we did *K9* in San Diego. And then after that, Universal said they'd never had a show run better than that and they said they wanted me to come in and head up Production.

I remember being called in for that meeting. I didn't know what the meeting was, I just knew to come in for a meeting. And I walked into the room and all of the hotshots were in the meeting. I walked in and said, "Whoa, the big kids are all here." And they thought that was cute.

But I mean, I had sweaty palms. I didn't expect to find the big kids all sitting there. And that's when they offered me the job. Terry Nelson was the gentleman who had had the position, and that was who I reported into during *K9*. I was very sensitive to that.

So when they said, "We want you to come head up Production," I said, "Replace Terry Nelson? No way. Not a chance."

So then I called my attorney and told him, "Guess what I just said 'no' to?" He's the one who stopped my clock. He said, "Donna, there's never been a woman who's had that job since Hollywood began. You can't say no." And I said, "Is that true?" And he said, "Absolutely it's true."

Then he said, "It's good you said no, because your price just doubled." That's the way attorneys think.

So I told them I really only wanted to do it for two years, because I'm a filmmaker now. I told them at Universal, "Guys, I don't want to wear pantyhose and work in the tower. Coming to work in an elevator and wearing pantyhose is so foreign to what I've been doing on the sets. I just can't imagine being a studio executive; I'm not interested in that at all."

Yet another job offer without writing up a resume.

DONNA: I've always been offered the job; I've never had to go interviewing for one. I always had offers, which is blessed.

This is the sad part: I only have men to thank, because there never was another woman who mentored me or promoted me or suggested me. There weren't women doing my job very much at that time, either. There were only like four and a half of us. And I'd have two of them come up to me on every job that I'd take (because I was always working) and say, "How the hell did you get this job? I was up for it too. Why are you getting all the work?" They'd be like that about it. And I'd say, "Look at your attitude. No wonder."

There was much more of a sense of wanting to push you out of your way instead of being your comrade.

But anytime I said "no" to a job, I always suggested women when I said "no" to a picture. If they got hired or not, that was up to them. That was one of my rules that I made for myself, that if I'm in a position of saying "no," I'm only going to suggest women. But it was not a long list.

But at Universal, I went there and was only going to stay two years and I was there for seven.

If you only wanted to do the job for two years, why did you stick around and do it for seven?

DONNA: I think because it was so challenging. It took me out of the 'on the set' atmosphere, but it was such a big, big, big, big job and I loved the people I was working with. The internal Universal people, I really like them a lot.

The job was so big, it kept me traveling around the world, which I had started to do with the bond company and then with the movies I made. I liked that. I liked the lifestyle. It suited me. Some people couldn't stand to travel that much, but somehow it suited me.

I didn't necessarily want to do all that traveling; I needed to stay at my desk. But you have to go to the set. That was my way; maybe some people who ran studios would say, "Oh, I never go on the set." Or, "I never travel. I leave that to all of my underlings. I wouldn't think of doing that."

And I was just the opposite. I learned it at the bond company. And when I arrived on the set, I'd say to every single filmmaker, "You don't want to ever see me get off an airplane again." I'd say it with humor but also with great intent. In other words, if you mess up, I'll be back. Just hope you never see me again, because that means you're doing things right.

I would assign one of my production executives to each show. We always had six to eight movies going at a time; it was brutal. And I had three really good production executives and a staff. So you'd split it up and everybody had like three movies going at a time. They'd take care of them on a daily basis while I was dealing with the next batch that was coming up. And I was also Senior Vice President of Post-Production. It was such a big job.

How did you learn post-production?

DONNA: I did a movie called *Reckless*, with Aidan Quinn and Daryl Hannah. This was one of the movies I did with Scott Rudin. We shot it in West Virginia. I was Production Coordinator and I was wrapping things up and a guy named Bob Colesberry was the Post-Production Supervisor on it. And one day Scott said Bob Colesberry was leaving and that he wanted me to be post-production supervisor.

And I thought, "Well, I don't know post-production, but I will after doing it."

So I looked at Scott and said, "Okay, but don't even think about offering me less than what Bob Colesberry's making." And he said, "Okay, we'll talk tomorrow."

We talked the next day and he offered me less. And I remember standing there, saying to myself, "Hold or fold. Which is it going to be, hold or fold?" And I folded. I did take the job, because I knew I would learn post-production. But I signed on for less than Colesberry would have been making, totally because I was a woman.

I wanted to be so stubborn and take a hike, but I knew I'd learn post-production. So I took it.

And then it did pay off, because then on *The Terminator* I did post-production, and then at Universal (big as that was) I had post-production on my slate as well.

Then you got back into completion bond work, right?

DONNA: Yes. While I was at Universal, this gentleman called me from Chicago and said he'd like to fly out. "I'm going to take the company jet," is what he said, "and fly out to meet you."

He was a big muckety-muck at CNA, a big insurance company. His name was Bernie and he flew out and I met with him and just thought he was charming and wonderful. CNA had never been in the entertainment business in any way. They were frightened of it, they didn't want to do it, they had no interest in it, but they were going to join Aeon, the world's largest insurance brokerage company out of Chicago. So they said they wanted me to head up this company, a bond company and an insurance company.

So I talked to them seriously, because I was getting burned out at Universal. I had just finished Waterworld, which was a nightmare. Bernie said "You can name the company."

And so I named the company -- I loved the name -- I named it Entertainment Coalition. I thought it was a wonderful name, because it covered the fact that we would be the insurance company for all the movies that we were doing, as well as be the bond company, so it was a company with two divisions.

So I left Universal and went right into Entertainment Coalition.

Can we back up to *Waterworld* for just a moment? I remember you saying once that when you put the budget together for that movie, the Powers That Be said you were crazy, that it would never cost that much. And, in the end, your budget estimate was pretty close to the final cost, right?

DONNA: I was a million off. Only one million off. And I've got to tell you, on that kind of movie, that's a nickel.

Thank God I did one of those cover-your-ass memos that outlined it all. I said we're not going to have it on time, do not plan to distribute it -- because that's going to be the biggest faux pas of all, there's nothing like advertising and getting ready for a big release -- because it won't be ready. It's really going to cost this much, second unit is going to go this long and cost this much, and yada, yada, yada. My crystal ball was working on that one, it really was.

So, let me ask you this. You started in 1978, we're talking now in 2008, so you've been at this for 30 years. Looking back, how have things changed for women? Are they better, worse, or about the same?

DONNA: I think it's quite status quo.

There are more female directors now. There are more female Production Managers. There are more writers, but I really don't think writing is a gender job. They're not management.

How would you define management?

DONNA: Someone like a studio executive, managing the movie. A Production Manager managing the movie. Anyone who's in the position of physically getting the movie made. Knowing how all the nuts and bolts work to make a movie, compared to writing a movie.

You can write a movie and it can be crisp and wonderful, but somebody's got to decide, "Are we going to start shooting this on a Tuesday on the corner of Westwood and Wilshire? Or are we going to shoot it on Monday, downtown on Sixth and Spring Street?"

It's that kind of magic about making the movie that I am so enamored with, really good at, and I'm pompous enough now to say that nobody can fool me about making a movie.

I've done 157 movies. I'd never counted them, but my secretary counted them one day and listed them all. But, when you're at the bond company, you might do 58 movies. And at Universal I probably did 99 movies, I don't know. But cumulatively, it's 157.

So what advice would you give someone starting out now?

DONNA: Well, I'm of the opinion that school is not going to get you into the movie business, especially into physical production. I don't think you can learn it in school.

I do a lot of speeches and I love doing that, and I tell classrooms the same thing: "Here I am, your guest tonight, and I love talking to you. How many of you want to be a director?" And eighty percent of the hands go up. "How many of you want to be writers?" Three percent of the hands go up. "How many of you want to be Line Producers?" No hands go up.

Then I say, "Who knows what a Line Producer is?" And there's utter silence.

Then I say, "Why do you think your teacher is here teaching moviemaking? Because your teacher failed. Your teacher couldn't make it in the business."

Do you get asked back often?

DONNA: Yes. But it's true, it's just too tough.

On *Raging Bull* I had sixteen Production Assistants. That's a lot. And I rotated them every week. One week you're with sound, the next week you're in the office, the next week you're with transportation, the next week you're with camera. Those sixteen kids, every one of them had a career after that movie.

So that became my system after discovering it on *Raging Bull.* I just made it up. And I did that on every movie: I'd hire the Production Assistants and then rotate them and give them a real taste of it. And then they find out, are you good at accounting? Are you good at camera? Most everybody wants to be on the set, and I'd keep saying,

"No. You've got to be in the office. You've got to learn the paperwork first. And then you'll get on the set. But you've got to learn the paperwork."

The DGA has a training program, so you go and take the test -- because anybody can take the test -- and then it's the six people out of four thousand who get the highest marks who get the chance at being hired. It's a big long shot, but it's another way in.

It's a very hard thing to tell people how to do it, how to get in.

What's life like for you now?

DONNA: When my husband died it really changed my life and I changed, also, because of it. I just didn't want to work that hard anymore. I'm still very much a part of Hollywood, but now I have a ranch.

Two years ago I bought a ranch an hour outside of Los Angeles, in a beautiful area. It's five acres, not a big deal but just right. It's total tranquility and harmony. I have three goats, which I think is a hoot. I don't know anything about goats, but I have three of them now. It's an hour out of LA, so when I go in I never go in before ten in the morning, so there's no traffic.

I'm doing just the tasty things I want to do instead of running things. I don't want to run things anymore.

FAST, CHEAP AND WRITTEN THAT WAY

FAST, CHEAP AND WRITTEN THAT WAY

Top Screenwriters on Writing for Low-Budget Movies

Hollywood's top screenwriters look back at their early low-budget efforts and provide valuable tips, tricks, and advice on how to create a solid screenplay for a low-budget movie.

Includes in-depth interviews with: Tom DiCillo (Living in Oblivion), Whit Stillman (Metropolitan), Richard Glatzer (Grief), Henry Jaglom (Venice/Venice), Dan Futterman (Capote), John McNaughton (Henry: Portrait of a Serial Killer), Coleman Hough (Bubble), Rebecca Miller (Personal Velocity), Stuart Gordon (Re-Animator), Joan Micklin Silver (Hester Street), Ali Selim (Sweet Land), Stephen Belber (Tape), Eric Bogosian (subUrbia), George Romero (Martin), Bob Clark (Children Shouldn't Play With Dead Things), Roger Nygard (Suckers), Alex Cox (Repo Man), Amy Holden Jones (Love Letters), Kenneth Lonergan (You Can Count On Me), Dylan Kidd (Roger Dodger), LM Kit Carson (Paris, Texas), Kasi Lemmons (Eve's Bayou), and Miranda July (Me and You and Everyone We Know).

Grab it today!

https://www.albertsbridgebooks.com

GET YOUR FREE ELI MARKS SHORT STORY BUNDLE

The Eli Marks Short Mystery Bundle
"The Invisible Assistant" & "The Last Customer"
Two short-story cozy mysteries in one!

"You will just LOVE these books."– VANISH Magazine

The Invisible Assistant

There's no question it was murder. But who killed whom?

What begins as a typical corporate event for magician Eli Marks turns into a twisted mystery when he is called to the site of a recent murder/suicide. Confronted by the details of the grisly crime scene,

Eli must sort through the post-mortem clues - and the bickering of the officials as well as a poorly-timed allergy attack - to determine just who murdered whom.

The Last Customer

The request was a first for Eli Marks: "Can you help me make my tuba disappear?"

Magician (and magic shop owner) Eli Marks is confronted with this odd demand just before he is about to close up shop for the day. Over the next few tense minutes, he finds a solution to that question which also, fortunately, puts him the positive side of what turns out to be a life-or-death situation.

Go to www.elimarksmysteries.com

GET YOUR FREE COMO LAKE PLAYERS SHORT MYSTERY

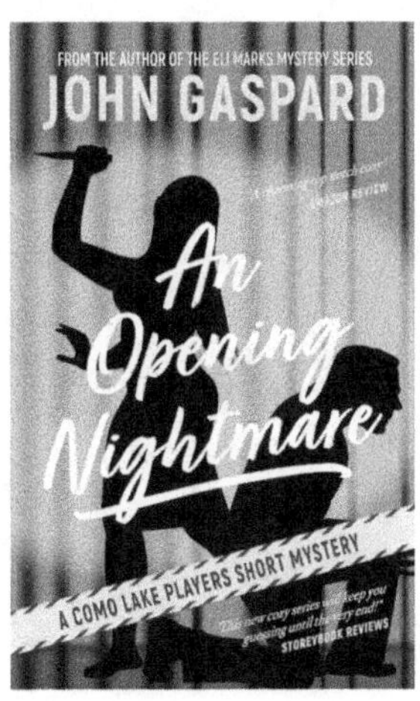

An Opening Nightmare

A Como Lake Players Short Mystery

A Killer Show, With the Corpses To Prove It

When an audience member is stabbed in the middle of an Opening Night performance, Leah must figure out who this clever killer is ... and make sure they don't kill the run of her show! Or murder her, as well!

A great introduction to The Como Lake Players mystery series: New Executive Director (and former actress) Leah Sexton must navigate the twisty world of community theater while dealing with crazy Board members, egomaniacal directors, self-centered actors ... and the occasional cold-blooded killer.

"This new cozy series will keep you guessing until the very end!" — Storeybook Reviews

https://www.albertsbridgebooks.com

THE AMBITIOUS CARD

AN ELI MARKS MYSTERY

THE AMBITIOUS CARD
An Eli Marks Mystery (#1)
The life of a magician isn't all kiddie shows and card tricks.
Sometimes it's murder. Especially when magician Eli Marks very
publicly debunks a famed psychic, and said psychic ends up dead.
The evidence, including a bloody King of Diamonds playing card
(one from Eli's own Ambitious Card routine), directs the police right
to Eli.

As more psychics are slain, and more King cards rise to the top, Eli can't escape suspicion. Things get really complicated when romance blooms with a beautiful psychic, and Eli discovers she's the next target for murder, and he's scheduled to die with her. Now Eli must use every trick he knows to keep them both alive and reveal the true killer.

Grab this fun and funny mystery today!
https://www.elimarksmysteries.com

ACTING CAN BE MURDER

A COMO LAKE PLAYERS MYSTERY
(BOOK ONE)

The Phrase "Dying On Stage"
Takes on a Whole New Meaning

After fleeing a failed relationship in New York, actress Leah Sexton finds herself as the new Executive Director of the Como Lake Players–a small community theater nestled in a sleepy St. Paul neighborhood. The initial calm of this new position is shattered immediately when a local critic–who had just panned the theater's latest production–is found murdered on the show's set.

On the heels of this grisly discovery, the show's lead actress tumbles down a flight of stairs–or was she pushed? In order to keep the show running and the theater afloat, Leah offers to step into the leading role. The arrival of her ex-boyfriend amid anonymous threats against her and the show require Leah to act as if her life depends on it. Because it does.

(Previously released under the pen name Bobbie Raymond)

Grab this funny, twisty mystery today!
https://www.albertsbridgebooks.com

THE SWORD & MR. STONE

A Wild Modern-Day Quest for King Arthur's Magical Sword, Excalibur!

Insurance adjuster Edward Stone's quiet life is completely upset when he's drawn into a wild search for King Arthur's fabled lost sword, Excalibur.

From the towering monuments of Stonehenge to the dark mists of Loch Ness, Stone finds himself battling evil forces intent upon possessing this long-lost treasure.

It's only when he embraces the magical nature of the legend that's
Stone is finally able to harness the epic forces behind Excalibur, the
Sword of Power.

*"A hero is no braver than an ordinary man, but he is brave five minutes
longer." — Ralph Waldo Emerson*

Grab this funny, gripping adventure today!
https://www.albertsbridgebooks.com

THE GREYHOUND OF THE BASKERVILLES

A new take on the Arthur Conan Doyle's classic mystery, "The Hound of the Baskervilles."

Think you know this story? Well, you haven't experienced it until you've read it through the eyes of Sherlock's pet dog.

It's the classic tale, now narrated by a dog. A greyhound, in fact, named Septimus.

Holmes and Watson ... and Septimus ... are called to the Baskerville estate to protect the new Baron and see if there is any truth to the legend of the hound of the Baskervilles. It's a dog-meet-dog mystery as Septimus sniffs out the clues, detects the red herrings and goes head-to-head with the monsterous creature which is haunting the moors.

It's the classic you love ... but now it's a slightly different tail!

"A delightful tale, familiar and yet filled with surprises."

Grab it now!

★ ★ ★ ★ ★

https://www.albertsbridgebooks.com

THE RIPPEROLOGISTS

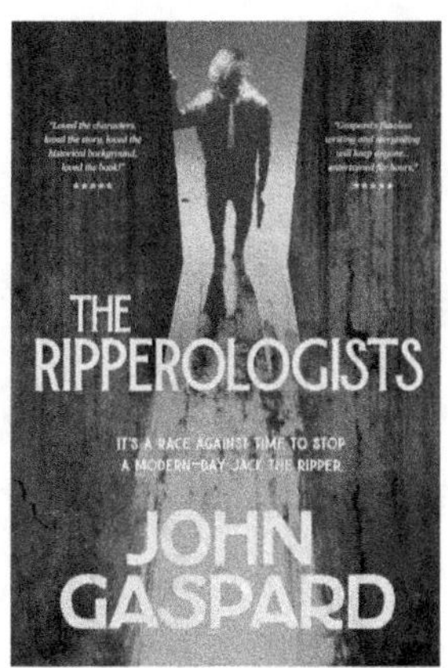

"Who are you?"

"For tonight, you can call me Jack. Mind if I come in?"

"Fascinating, couldn't put it down!"

Nunes, Amazon.com (verified purchase)

★★★★★

When a copycat serial killer begins recreating Jack the Ripper's 1888 murder spree, two competing experts are forced to work together to stop him.

What they don't understand is that his murderous spree is far more personal than either of them ever suspected.

Grab this electrifying race-against-time mystery/thriller today!

https://www.albertsbridgebooks.com

BOOKS BY JOHN GASPARD

The Como Lake Players Mysteries
ACTING CAN BE MURDER
DYING TO AUDITION
REHEARSED TO DEATH

The Eli Marks Mystery Series
THE AMBITIOUS CARD (#1)
THE BULLET CATCH (#2)
THE MISER'S DREAM (#3)
THE LINKING RINGS (#4)
THE FLOATING LIGHT BULB (#5)
THE ZOMBIE BALL (#6)
THE MAGIC SQUARE (#7)
THE SELF-WORKING TRICK (#8)

Stand-Alone Novels
THE SWORD & MR. STONE
A CHRISTMAS CARL
THE GREYHOUND OF THE BASKERVILLES
THE RIPPEROLOGISTS

Filmmaking Books
FAST, CHEAP AND UNDER CONTROL
FAST, CHEAP AND WRITTEN THAT WAY
TELL THEM IT'S A DREAM SEQUENCE
WOMEN MAKE MOVIES

ABOUT THE AUTHOR

John is author of the Eli Marks mystery series as well as four other stand-alone novels, *"The Sword & Mr. Stone," "A Christmas Carl," " The Greyhound of the Baskervilles"* and *"The Ripperologists."*

He also writes the *Como Lake Players* mystery series.

In real life, John's not a magician, but he has directed six low-budget features that cost very little and made even less—that's no small trick.

He's also written books on the subject of low-budget filmmaking. Ironically, they've made more than the films. Those books (*"Fast, Cheap and Under Control"* and *"Fast, Cheap and Written That Way"*) are available in eBook, Paperback and audiobook formats.

John lives in Minnesota and shares his home with his lovely wife, several dogs, a few cats and a handful of pet allergies.

Find out more at: https://www.albertsbridgebooks.com and https://www.elimarksmysteries.com.

facebook.com/JohnGaspardAuthorPage

twitter.com/johngaspard

instagram.com/johngaspard

bookbub.com/authors/john-gaspard